ROYAL WARSHIPS

PAUL BEAVER

A handy pocket guide to all
major vessels currently in service.

MODERN
ROYAL NAVY
WARSHIPS

PAUL BEAVER

Patrick Stephens
Wellingborough, Northamptonshire

© Paul Beaver 1987.
Drawings © Bob Downey and Ian Sturton 1987

First published 1987

British Library Cataloguing in Publication Data

Beaver, Paul
Modern Royal Navy Warships.
1. Great Britain. *Royal Navy*   2. Warships
— Great Britain
I. Title
623.8'25'0941   VA454

ISBN 0-85059-861-3

Cover illustrations: Front *'Leander' Class frigates make up
the most successful group of British warships built since the
Second World War: with special modifications they will remain
in service until the mid 1990s. This is HMS* Charybdis *(F75)
from the Batch 3 'Seawolf' group (FPU).* **Back** *Still vital to the
defence of British interests, the conventional submarine is
small but potent. This is an 'O' boat returning from patrol
(FPU).*

*Patrick Stephens is part of the
Thorsons Publishing Group*

Printed and bound in Great Britain.

CONTENTS

Introduction 6
Aircraft carriers 8
Assault ships 13
Ballistic missile submarines 16
Fleet submarines 19
Conventional submarines 27
Guided missile destroyers 37
Frigates 51
Mines counter-measure vessels 82
Mines counter-measure support ship 96
Offshore patrol vessels 98
Survey craft 111
Diving support and seabed operations ships 118
Training craft 122
Appendix 1: Naval sensors and sonars 127
Appendix 2: Royal Naval aircraft 129
Index 135

INTRODUCTION

The Royal Navy is today primarily an anti-submarine force with a substantial ability to operate outside the North Atlantic Treaty Organization's area of interest. In the last decade, the Falklands' conflict from April to July 1982 proved to be the most important post-Second World War event and reinforced belief in the Fleet's need to be able to operate against a powerful opposing force with its own land-based air power. Although four major surface combat units—two guided missile destroyers and two general purpose frigates—were lost to enemy air action, the conflict provided valuable experience for the Royal Navy.

Much of that experience has been funnelled into the design and equipment of new warships like the Type 22 and Type 23 now building in yards around the United Kingdom. There have been numerous changes introduced since the Falklands including the provision of more and better weapon systems, advanced radar with moving target indication and better internal construction.

Modern Royal Naval warships will almost certainly be equipped with a point defence missile system (like Vertical Launched Sea Wolf) or a close-in weapons system (like Goalkeeper or Phalanx); in addition, the need for providing naval gunfire support for shore bombardment to support the ground forces was confirmed and new warships will be armed with a conventional dual-purpose gun mounting. For over-the-horizon anti-ship operations, in self-defence as well as for offensive operations, longer range missiles are being fitted including the American Harpoon system in the Type 23 frigate.

Modern radars from British manufacturers are being tested and delivered to shipyards in the latter half of the decade, including the first 3-D system since the days of conventional aircraft carriers fifteen to twenty years ago. More importantly, ways have been found of defeating the radars and identification systems of potentially hostile radars using chaff and active decoys. Even with the development of supersonic sea-skimming missiles, countermeasures against advanced anti-ship weapons should prove reliable until the missiles inevitably take the upper hand of technology again. Most new warships will also carry two Lynx helicopters, providing better long-range surveillance capabilities, thus allowing the parent ship to remain out of range of enemy missile and gun systems whilst a target is being positively identified. In overall terms, the introduction of the airborne early warning variant of the Sea King should prevent *Sheffield*-type disasters in the future.

6

It is the design of modern Royal Naval warships which should prove to be the most important development of the post-Falklands era, including the provision of low-radar contour superstructures using non-vertical sides and soft angles to give the smallest radar reflective surface possible. Much work has been carried out by Swan Hunter, Vosper Thornycroft and Yarrow on the prefabrication of modern warships, thus reducing building times and relative costs. Internally, poly-vinyl sheeting around electrical circuits, which caused the spread of toxic fumes when *Sheffield* burned, has been replaced by a softer alternative and the impact resistance of the deck (floor) and bulkhead (wall) covering has been improved to prevent injuries being inflicted from blast damage or internal explosions. As a result of the Falklands, the Royal Navy is better prepared to defend British maritime interests.

During the preparation of this book, I have been considerably assisted by the Director of Public Relations (Royal Navy), Captain Guy Liardet, CBE, and his staff; by the various Command and Staff Public Relations Officers; by the Officer-in-Charge of the Fleet Photographic Unit, Lieutenant Commander Rod Safe; ship's public relations officers Commander William Bowman *(Illustrious)* and Commander Peter Nicholas *(Invincible)*; the public relations staff of Swan Hunter and Vosper Thornycroft; and by my friends and colleagues Mike Lennon and Robin Walker. The drawings were prepared by the late Bob Downey and Ian Sturton. However, having said all that, any errors in or interpretations of the facts are mine alone. For more details about the whole structure, equipment and workings of the Royal Navy, the reader is urged to consult the *Encyclopaedia of the Modern Royal Navy*, third edition, and for more details on the missile systems, *British Military Missiles* in this series.

Paul Beaver
October 1986

AIRCRAFT CARRIERS
'Invincible' Class CVS

Name *Invincible*; **Pennant number** R05; **Flight deck code** N; **Standard displacement** 16,000 tons; **Full displacement** 19,810 tons; **Length (overall)** 206.6 m; **Length (waterline)** 192.9 m; **Beam (flight deck)** 31.9 m; **Beam (waterline)** 27.5 m; **Draught** 7.3 m; **Propulsion** 4 × RR Olympus TM3B gas turbines (112,000 shp) driving two shafts; **Range** 5,000 nm at 18 kt; **Speed (max)** 28 kt; **Speed (cruising)** 18 kt; **Complement** 131 officers, 869 ratings (excl air group); **Armament** 1 × 2 Sea Dart SAM launchers, 2 × 20 mm Phalanx (later 3 × Goalkeeper) CIWS, 2 × 20 mm Oerlikon GAM-B01, SRBOC and Corvus CM launchers; **Sensors** 2 × 1006, 2 × 909, 1 × 992R, 1 × 1022, electronic warfare and direction finding equipment, SCOT; **Sonar** 1 × 2016; **Aircraft** 20 max, usually 5 × Sea Harrier FRS 1, 9 × Sea King HAS 5; **Builders** Vickers (Barrow); **Laid down** 20 July 1973; **Launched** 3 May 1977; **Accepted/Completed** 19 March 1980; **Commissioned** 11 July 1980; **Refits** 1982, 1986–87.

Name *Illustrious*; **Pennant number** R06; **Flight deck code** L; **Builders** Swan Hunter; **Laid down** 7 October 1976; **Launched** 1 December 1978; **Completed** 18 June 1982; **Formally accepted** 20 June 1982; **Re-dedicated** 30 March 1983; **Aircraft** Includes provision for 4 × Sea King AEW 3; **Refit** 1988 (planned).

Name *Ark Royal*; **Pennant number** R07; **Flight deck code** R; **Length overall** 209.1 m; **Beam (flight deck)** 35 m; **Armament** Includes 3 × CIWS, 2 × Sea Gnat chaff dispensers and 2 × 2 30 mm Oerlikon GCM; **Builders** Swan Hunter; **Laid down** 14 December 1978; **Launched** 2 June 1981; **Completed** October 1984; **Accepted** 1 July 1985; **Commissioned** 1 November 1985.

The first aircraft carrier to be designed, ordered and built after the Second World War started life as an anti-submarine cruiser design with the express purpose of taking a large number, up to ten, of medium anti-submarine helicopters to sea and acting as a command and control ship for a naval task group. The original plan was for a 12,500-ton ship with a hangar in the island structure. By the late 1960s, the design had changed to that of 'through deck cruiser' at 17,500 tons, carrying twelve Sea King-type helicopters and mounting Sea Wolf as well as the Sea Dart area defence missile system.

By April 1973, when the first 'cruiser' was ordered from Vickers, the design changes had included the abandonment of the Sea Wolf system, with the future ships of the new class relying on the air defence of escort destroyers instead. Another new factor was the possibility of carrying vertical take-off and landing (VTOL) aircraft, thus requiring a full length flight deck, hangar below the flight deck and eventually a seven-degree ski-jump type take-off ramp for'ard. The Sea Harrier was considered part of the ship's complement from May 1975.

Invincible commenced builder's sea trials in April 1979 and the first Royal Naval acceptance trials were completed in the winter of 1980/

Below left *After special trials,* Invincible *entered refit in April 1986 for modernization to the standards of her later sister ships; she is pictured here during full speed trials in 1984* (RN/PO Phot Kent).

Below Illustrious *in home waters with her fifteen embarked Sea Kings flying by, including three airborne early warning types (left) and two in experimental light colours* (RN/HMS *Illustrious*).

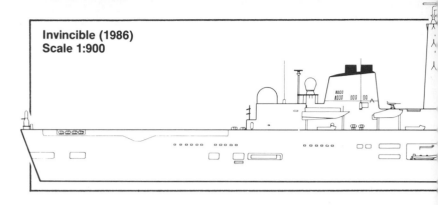

Invincible (1986)
Scale 1:900

81, allowing the ship to deploy to the Western Atlantic in 1981. It was a brief spell of action in 1982 which provided the ship and the concept with its greatest and totally unforeseen test, following the Argentine invasion of the Falkland Islands and South Georgia. In 1975–76, plans were made to allow the ship to carry a Royal Marine Commando group for quick-dash and use was made of this facility during Operation 'Corporate'.

The Royal Navy's Task Force was led by the aircraft carrier *Hermes* (de-commissioned in 1984), with *Invincible* providing slightly less than fifty per cent of the Sea Harrier air defence. During the conflict, the ship spent 166 continuous days at sea, steaming 51,660 nm and spending 273 hours at action stations. The nine Sea King HAS 5 helicopters embarked flew 4,700 hours and the eight Sea Harriers (three additional to the peacetime complement) were airborne for 1,580 hours. The ship remained in the South Atlantic until relieved by

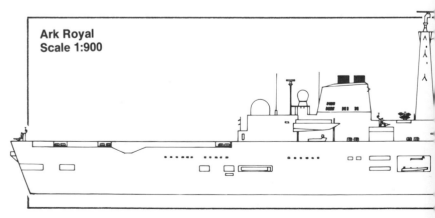

Ark Royal
Scale 1:900

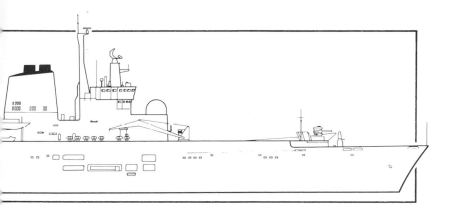

Illustrious in August, both ships meeting for the first time in the Falkland Islands' Protection Zone.

After a post-operational refit, which included the fitting of the American Phalanx close-in weapon system and other self-defence equipment, *Invincible* was made ready to be flagship of the 1983–84 Far Eastern Deployment, called Orient Express. The remainder of 1984 was spent on exercise and flag-showing and *Invincible* undertook six major NATO exercises. In January 1986, however, the ship was re-designated as the Dartmouth Training Ship, with her air group being embarked in her sister ship *Ark Royal*, and she entered refit in late 1986. The refit includes the upgrading of the crew and aircraft accommodation, new sensors and communications gear, provision to carry Sea King AEW 2 helicopters, the Phalanx replaced by Goalkeeper CIWS and a twelve-degree ski-jump.

Second of the '*Invincible*' Class CVSs, *Illustrious* had a remarkable

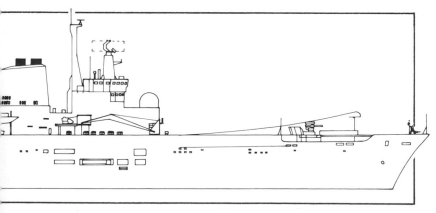

Ark Royal *enters Portsmouth in July 1985, prior to the fitting of the close-range defensive armament. Note the Sea Harrier FRS 1 and Swordfish on deck* (RN/Fleet Photographic Unit).

early life, being completed by the shipbuilders for service nearly a year ahead of schedule in order that she could be ready to operate in the South Atlantic. A rapid series of sea trials and shake-down followed her departure from Tyneside in June 1982, including the fitting of the Phalanx CIWS at Portsmouth. Aircraft were embarked and the ship declared operationally ready by 2 August, with her air complement including two hastily converted Sea King helicopters equipped with the Thorn EMI Electronics Searchwater airborne early warning radar.

Illustrious was deployed to the South Atlantic between August and December 1982, actually leaving the FIPZ in late October and returning via exercises with the US Navy off Florida. 1983 and 1984 were spent in exercises with NATO forces (during which time a Sea Harrier from the ship successfully completed an emergency landing on a Spanish coaster), and in 1985 the first front-line AEW in the Fleet Air Arm for nearly seven years was embarked for the first time. In July 1986, the ship set out on the around-the-world group deployment as flagship. She is scheduled for refit to *Ark Royal* standard in 1988, although her CIWS system may be upgraded before then.

To have originally been named *Indomitable*, *Ark Royal* (V) was completed four and a half months ahead of schedule, although the gun armament was added at Portsmouth, the warship's base port. The full work-up was undertaken in the spring of 1986 and it is reported that Plessey Type 996 radar will be fitted in due course. Because of the lack of a third carrier air group, the Sea Harrier and Sea King group from *Invincible* embarked in April 1986, together with a newly formed flight of Sea King AEW 2 helicopters.

ASSAULT SHIPS

'Fearless' Class

Name *Fearless*; **Pennant number** L10; **Flight deck code** FS; **Standard displacement** 11,060 tons; **Full displacement** 12,120 tons (16,950 tons in full ballast); **Length overall** 158.5 m; **Beam** 24.4 m; **Draught** 7.0 m forward / 9.8 m aft; **Propulsion** 2 × English Electric turbines (22,000 shp) with 2 shafts; **Range** 5,000 nm at 20 kt; **Speed** 21 kt; **Complement** 37 officers and 500 ratings, 80 RM for landing craft and beach unit (150 cadets carried in Dartmouth Training Ship role); **Armament** 4 × 4 Seacat launchers, 2 × 40 mm Bofors Mk 9 GP guns (to be replaced by 2 × 20 mm Oerlikon GAM-B01); **Sensors** 1 × 978 and 1 × 994 radars, electronic warfare equipment, radio direction finding and SCOT; **Aircraft** Provision for four support helicopters; **Landing craft** 4 × LCVP, 4 × LCU; **Builders** Harland & Wolff; **Laid down** 25 July 1962; **Launched** 19 December 1963; **Completed** 1965; **Commissioned** 25 November 1965.

Fearless *at sea during a transit to an amphibious exercise — note the large flight deck but no hangar* (RN).

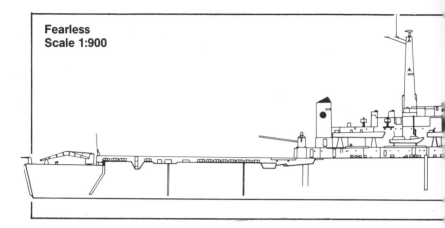

Fearless
Scale 1:900

Name *Intrepid*; **Pennant number** L11; **Flight deck code** IS; **Armament** 2 × 20 mm Oerlikon GAM-B01 & 2 × 30 mm GCM replace Bofors, 2 × Seacat only; **Builders** John Brown; **Laid down** 19 December 1962; **Launched** 25 June 1964; **Completed** 1966; **Commissioned** 11 March 1967.

The Class was built to provide the Royal Navy with the ability to carry out amphibious operations on either of the NATO flanks and to act as command, control and communications (C^3) ships during the landing phase. The ships were designed with large vehicle decks and a dry dock installation for carrying large landing craft (LCUs); small LCVPs are carried on davits. The upper open tank deck was converted to take on the role of helicopter landing deck during the design stage, but there are no undercover facilities for maintaining helicopters.

The two ships of the Class are earmarked to support the Royal Marine Commandos in wartime, and have acted in a similar role for Out of Area operations, as during Operation 'Corporate' (1982). The ships are very versatile and have accommodation for up to 700 RM Commandos, or they can be used for emergency evacuation of civilians and disaster relief. In peacetime, one ship acts as Dartmouth Training Ship while the other is laid up in refit or reserve.

In 1992, the ships will reach the end of their useful lives and must be replaced if the credibility of the amphibious concept is to be maintained. A new design would need adequate accommodation for helicopters which operate in support of the embarked Royal Marine Commandos.

Intrepid was used for the first seaborne trials of the SCOT (satellite communications onboard terminal) system for advanced global communications.

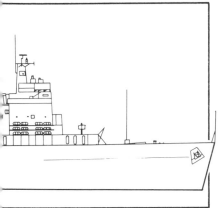

Intrepid *in the role of Dartmouth Training Ship, prior to the fitting of Oerlikon GAM-B01 guns and SCOT terminals* (RN).

BALLISTIC MISSILE SUBMARINES

'Resolution' Class

Name *Resolution*; **Pennant number** S22; **Surface displacement** 7,500 tons; **Full displacement** 8,400 tons (dived); **Length (overall)** 129.5 m; **Beam** 10.1 m; **Draught** 9.1 m; **Propulsion** 1 × pressurized water nuclear reactor and geared turbines (15,000 shp), 1 × shaft; **Speed** 25 kt (dived), 20 kt (surfaced); **Complement** 13 officers and 130 ratings (port and starboard crew); **Armament** 16 × Polaris SLBM, 6 × 53 cm bow torpedo tubes; **Sensors** 1 × Search radar; **Sonars** 1 × 2001, 1 × 2007; **Builders** Vickers (Barrow); **Laid down** 26 February 1964; **Launched** 15 September 1966; **Completed** 1967; **Commissioned** 2 October 1967.

Name *Repulse*; **Pennant number** S23; **Laid down** 12 March 1965; **Launched** 4 November 1967; **Completed** 1968; **Commissioned** 28 September 1968.

Name *Renown*; **Pennant number** S26; **Laid down** 25 June 1964; **Launched** 25 February 1967; **Completed** 1968; **Commissioned** 15 November 1968.

Name *Revenge*; **Pennant number** S27; **Builders** Cammell Laird; **Laid down** 19 May 1965; **Launched** 15 March 1968; **Completed** 1969; **Commissioned** 4 December 1969.

Replacement design The Trident design which will replace the *'Resolution'* Class calls for a boat of 15,000 tons displacement, a length of 150 m, beam of 12.8 m and a pressurized water reactor; Vickers (Barrow) will build all four of the boats ordered.

The 'R' boats — known as 'bomber boats' to their crews — were designed to take the British independent nuclear deterent to sea, as a result of the Nassau convention and the British Government's decision to transfer the strategic nuclear role to the Royal Navy from

R Class SSBN
Scale 1:900

Renown *enters the Clyde Submarine base in January 1981* (RN).

the Royal Air force's V-Bomber force. The four boats in commission have the duty of maintaining the sixteen American-built A3 Polaris missiles with their British-built warheads ready to fire in the event of attack on the United Kingdom. The missiles are fired beneath the water and the guidance requirements of each missile are calculated by two high speed computers; to ensure that they are correct, the target information is fed into one and the other checks it for accuracy in thirty milliliseconds; the missile still requires the Captain's permission to fire before the boat's weapons officer can launch the system.

Like its American and French counterparts, a British SSBN (nuclear-powered ballistic missile submarine) has two complete crews, the Port and Starboard, who take the submarine to sea alternately on a patrol which can last about three months; when not aboard, the spare crew takes leave and works in the submarine facility at Faslane in Scotland.

Navigation is by means of the submarine inertial navigation system (SINS), dead reckoning, Decca Navigator, satellite navigation (Global Positioning System) and perhaps the use of underwater signal buoys. Communications when on patrol can be achieved by trailing a long-line radio antenna for low frequency radio transmissions. This system would be used in wartime to pass the Prime Minister's decision to use Polaris. 'R' boats come under command of CINCFLEET

Trident Class SSBN
Scale 1:900

Still highly effective although now coming to the end of a useful career providing the United Kingdom with a strategic deterrence capability, the 'Resolution' *Class SSBN* Revenge (RN/HMS Neptune).

(Commander-in-Chief Fleet) at Northwood, near London.

Besides the Polaris missiles, the submarines are armed with Mk 8 and Mk 24 Tigerfish torpedoes for self-defence and perhaps even offensive action should they be required to do so. In 1982, *Renown* became the first SSBN to become operational with the Polaris warhead update, known as Chevaline, tests having been carried out on the American Eastern Atlantic test range in January 1982. Chevaline is an interim update with three 60 kT MIRV (Multiple Independent Re-entry Vehicles) and it will remain service until the arrival of the Trident missile in the mid-1990s.

Considerable effort has been taken to ensure that the living accommodation aboard the boats is of a high standard bearing in mind the patrol routine and time spent at sea. Various onboard entertainment, study and recreational facilities have been designed into the boats. Accommodation is better than in most submarines, but not as good as in many surface ships.

The '*R*' Class boats have a useful life of about 25 years. The new class of Trident missile submarines, to be known as the '*Vanguard*' Class, were ordered in 1986.

FLEET SUBMARINES
'Trafalgar' Class

Name *Trafalgar*; **Pennant number** S107; **Surface displacement** 4,730 tons; **Full displacement** 5,200 tons (dived); **Length** 85.4 m; **Beam** 9.83 m, **Draught** 9.5 m; **Propulsion** 1 × pressurized water reactor, 2 × General Electric steam turbines (15,000 shp), 2 × Paxman auxiliary diesels (4,000 shp), 1 × shaft; **Speed** 30+ kt (dived); **Complement** 12 officers and 85 ratings; **Armament** 5 × 53 cm forward torpedo tubes (Sub-Harpoon carried); **Sensors** 1 × 1006; **Sonars** 1 × 183, 1 × 2007, 1 × 2020, 1 × 2024 TA; **Builders** Vickers; **Laid down** 1978; **Launched** 1 July 1981; **Completed** 1983; **Commissioned** 27 May 1983.

Name *Turbulent*; **Pennant number** S87; **Laid down** 1979; **Launched** 1 December 1982; **Completed** 21 November 1983; **Commissioned** 28 April 1984.

Name *Tireless*; **Pennant number** S88; **Laid down** 1981; **Launched** 17 March 1984; **Completed** 1985; **Commissioned** 5 October 1985.

Name *Torbay*; **Pennant number** S90; **Laid down** December 1982; **Launched** 8 March 1985; **Completed** August 1986; **Commissioned** 1987.

Name *Trenchant*; **Pennant number** S91; **Laid down** April 1984; **Launched** November 1986; **Completed** 1988; **Commissioned** 1988.

Name *Talent*; **Pennant number** S92; **Laid down** 1985; **Launched** 1987; **Completed** 1989; **Commissioned** 1989.

Name *Triumph*; **Pennant number** S93; **Laid down** 1986; **Launched** 1988; **Completed** 1989; **Commissioned** 1990.

Amongst the newest and most deadly Fleet type submarines in commission is the 'Trafalgar' *Class, whose name ship is seen leaving Liverpool* (RN).

The nuclear-powered (but not nuclear-armed) Fleet submarine is the modern equivalent of a battleship and is the main striking power of the modern Royal Navy. It is also the single most effective anti-submarine unit available to the Commander-in-Chief Fleet.

Its main wartime role is to find and destroy enemy submarines and surface ships, but is is also capable of conducting an ocean-wide surveillance task using the sonar systems, linked to the onboard computers. Operating at depths below 500 m, boats of the '*Trafalgar*' Class are able to detect, track, identify and if necessary engage contacts before the enemy has had the opportunity to identify the presence of a submarine.

Weapons available include the Mk 8 unguided, free-running torpedo (the sort used to sink the Argentine cruiser *Belgrano*, when it posed a threat to the British forces off the Falkland Islands), the Mk 24 Tigerfish wire-guided torpedo and the McDonnell Douglas UGM-84B Sub-Harpoon system which is an encapsulated over-the-horizon cruise/sea skimming missile.

Thought to be the quietest SSN (nuclear-powered submarine) in service anywhere, *Turbulent* differs from her sister ship *Trafalgar*, and the previous and outwardly similar '*Swiftsure*' Class, in having considerable attention paid to silent running and noise reduction.

Usually SSNs remain submerged for much of their time at sea, but Turbulent *has surfaced for passage down the Irish Sea* (RN/HMS *Gannet*).

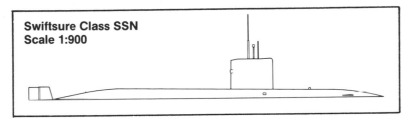

Swiftsure Class SSN
Scale 1:900

'Swiftsure' Class

Name *Swiftsure*; **Pennant number** S126; **Surface displacement** 4,400 tons; **Full displacement** 4,900 tons (dived); **Length** 82.9 m; **Beam** 9.8 m; **Draught** 8.2 m; **Propulsion** 1 × pressurized water reactor, 2 × General Electric steam turbines (15,000 shp), 2 × Paxman diesels (4,000 shp); **Speed** 30+ kt (dived); **Complement** 12 officers and 85 ratings; **Armament** 5 × 53 cm forward torpedo tubes; **Sensors** 1 × 1006, 1 × ESM; **Sonars** 1 × 183, 1 × 2001, 1 × 2007; **Builders** Vickers (Barrow); **Laid down** 15 April 1969; **Launched** 17 September 1971; **Completed** 1972; **Commissioned** 17 April 1973; **Refit** 1979–82.

Name *Sovereign*; **Pennant number** S108; **Laid down** 17 September 1970; **Launched** 17 February 1973; **Completed** 1974; **Commissioned** 11 July 1974.

Name *Superb*; **Pennant number** S109; **Laid down** 16 March 1972; **Launched** 30 November 1974; **Completed** 1976; **Commissioned** 13 November 1976; **Refit** 1982–85.

Name *Sceptre*; **Pennant number** S104; **Laid down** 25 October 1973; **Launched** 20 November 1976; **Completed** 1977; **Commissioned** 14 February 1978.

Name *Spartan*; **Pennant number** S105; **Laid down** 24 April 1976; **Launched** 7 December 1978; **Completed** 1979; **Commissioned** 22 September 1979.

Name *Splendid*; **Pennant number** S106; **Laid down** 23 November 1977; **Launched** 5 October 1979; **Completed** December 1980; **Commissioned** 21 March 1981.

Designed to operate as long-range independent strike units of the Royal Navy, the '*Swiftsure*' Class SSNs have both anti-submarine and anti-surface vessel warfare roles, particularly with the introduction of the Mk 24 Tigerfish Mod 1 and the UGM-84B Sub-Harpoon into service; by 1990, the Spearfish heavyweight torpedo will be in service as well.

The Admiralty changed the design of this class to make them wider, have a longer pressure hull, but shorter overall hull length than the previous *'Churchill'* and *'Valiant'* Classes. This has allowed the internal arrangement to be greatly improved and by the use of only five torpedo (now called weapons) tubes, the submarine is presumably allowed to dive deeper. The Royal Navy officially will only say that its submarines are capable of diving to depths in excess of 175 m (575 ft) but some estimates give depths three times that figure.

Accommodation is always cramped in submarines but greater

Below *Leaving Faslane on a cold morning,* Splendid *was the last of the 'S' boats to commission, having been built by Vickers at Barrow* (RN).

Bottom Swiftsure *showing her search periscope raised and the type 1006 navigation radar antenna on top of the fin. Note the nuclear safety boat in attendance* (RN/HMS Neptune).

Amongst the aerials which Superb *can raise is the cone-shaped wireless mast, seen behind an electronic warfare blister and the navigation radar* (RN/HMS *Neptune*).

efforts have been made in the nuclear-powered types because the patrol lengths are so long — at least 100 days if the boat is deployed to the South Atlantic, as one regularly is every three months or so. Navigation aids for such long voyages include the Decca Navigator, Submarine Intertial Naviation System (SINS) and the use of satellite navigation systems. Communications underwater can be achieved by underwater telephone (which is not considered secure) and by low frequency radio transmissions.

The pressurized water reactor system has the same core as earlier SSNs but the life of the system has been increased and the system generally improved especially for silent running routines.

'Churchill' Class

Name *Churchill*; **Pennant number** S46; **Standard displacement** 3,500 tons; **Full displacement** 4,800 tons (dived); **Length** 86.9 m; **Beam** 10.1 m; **Draught** 8.2 m; **Propulsion** 1 × pressurized water reactor, 2 × English Electric steam turbines (15,000 shp), 1 × shaft; **Speed** 28 kt (dived); **Complement** 13 officers and 90 ratings; **Armament** 6 × 53 cm forward torpedo tubes; **Sensors** 1 × 1006, 1 × ESM; **Sonars** 1 × 183, 1 × 2001; **Builders** Vickers (Barrow); **Laid down** 30 June 1967; **Launched** 20 December 1968; **Completed** 1970; **Commissioned** 15 July 1970.

Name *Courageous*; **Pennant numbers** 50; **Complement** 13 officers and 96 ratings; **Laid down** 15 May 1968; **Launched** 7 March 1970; **Completed** 1971; **Commissioned** 16 October 1971.

Name *Conqueror*; **Pennant number** S48; **Complement** 13 officers and 100 ratings; **Builders** Cammell Laird; **Laid down** 5 December 1967; **Launched** 18 August 1969; **Completed** 1971; **Commissioned** 9 November 1971; **Refits** 1975-77, 1982-83.

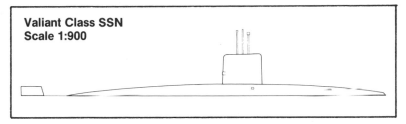

Valiant Class SSN
Scale 1:900

Left *One of the heroes of the Falklands,* Conqueror, *returns to Faslane after that long deployment to the South Atlantic. Note the casing party preparing to berth the boat* (RN).

Below left Churchill *launches the first live Sub-Harpoon missile for the Royal Navy at the American live firing range in 1981* (McDonnell Douglas).

'Valiant' Class

Name *Valiant*; **Pennant number** S102; **Standard displacement** 3,500 tons; **Full displacement** 4,500 tons (dived); **Length, Beam and Draught** as *Churchill*; **Propulsion** System and performance as *Churchill*; **Complement** 14 officers and 96 ratings; **Armament** as *Churchill*; **Sensors and Sonars** As *Churchill*; **Builders** Vickers (Barrow); **Laid down** 22 January 1962; **Launched** 3 December 1963; **Completed** 1966; **Commissioned** 18 July 1966.

Name *Warspite*; **Pennant number** S103; **Laid down** 10 December 1963; **Launched** 25 September 1965; **Completed** 1967; **Commissioned** 18 April 1967.

The first all-British nuclear-powered submarines, the '*Valiant*' Class and the later internally modified '*Churchill*' Class, followed the successful operational trials of *Dreadnought*, the first British-built (but American-powered) nuclear-powered Fleet submarine which was withdrawn from service in 1982.

Churchill carried out trials with the McDonnell Douglas Sub-Harpoon system in 1979–81 and the same boat was the last SSN to refit at Chatham, departing the Naval Base for the last on 7 May 1983.

Conqueror achieved world fame by sinking the Argentine cruiser, *General Belgrano*, which was threatening the British task force off the Falkland Islands in May 1982. The boat was also used previously for Mk 24 Tigerfish trials in 1978.

Valiant was at Singapore in 1967, returning to the United Kingdom after the deployment fully submerged for 28 days, a Royal Navy record. She was deployed East of Suez 1967–68 and 1974–75.

Above Valiant *is now the oldest British SSN in commission and is seen here in an Atlantic swell* (UK MoD).

Below *Departing for another cruise,* Warspite's *casing party prepare the boat for sea duty which could be of three months' duration* (RN/HMS *Neptune*).

CONVENTIONAL SUBMARINES
'Oberon' Class

Name *Odin*; **Pennant number** S10; **Standard displacement** 1,610 tons; **Full displacement** 2,410 tons (dived); **Length** 90 m; **Beam** 8.1 m; **Draught** 5.5 m; **Propulsion** 2 × Admiralty diesels (3,680 bhp), 2 × English Electric motors (6,000 shp), 2 × shafts; **Speed (surfaced)** 12 kt; **Speed (dived)** 17 kt; **Complement** 6 officers and 62 ratings; **Armament** 6 × 53 cm forward torpedo tubes, 2 × stern tubes; **Sensors** 1 × 1002; **Sonars** 1 × 187, 1 × 2007; **Builders** Cammell Laird; **Laid down** 27 April 1959; **Launched** 4 November 1960; **Completed** 1962; **Commissioned** 3 May 1962.

Name *Olympus*; **Pennant number** S12; **Builders** Vickers (Barrow); **Laid down** 4 March 1960; **Launched** 14 June 1961; **Completed** 1962; **Commissioned** 7 July 1962.

Name *Osiris*; **Pennant number** S13; **Builders** Vickers (Barrow); **Laid down** 26 January 1963; **Launched** 29 November 1962; **Completed** 1963; **Commissioned** 11 January 1964.

Name *Onslaught*; **Pennant number** S14; **Builders** HM Dockyard (Chatham); **Laid down** 8 April 1959; **Launched** 24 September 1960; **Completed** 1962; **Commissioned** 14 August 1962.

Odin, built by Cammell Laird, is the oldest 'Oberon' *Class conventional, diesel-electric submarine in commission* (RN/HMS *Neptune*).

Above *Preparing to dive,* Onyx *has her wireless mast and search periscope raised and her forward planes ready for manoeuvring (RN/HMS* Dolphin*).*

Below *Conventional submarines like* Otus *are young men's commands and despite modern equipment, the accommodation is still cramped in these boats (RN/HMS* Dolphin*).*

Ocelot *manoeuvres alongside the wall at* Dolphin (RN).

Name *Otter*; **Pennant number** S15; **Builders** Scotts; **Laid down** 14 January 1960; **Launched** 15 May 1961; **Completed** 1962; **Commissioned** 20 August 1962.

Name *Oracle*; **Pennant number** S16; **Builders** Cammell Laird; **Laid down** 26 April 1960; **Launched** 26 September 1961; **Completed** 1963; **Commissioned** 14 February 1963.

Name *Ocelot*; **Pennant number** S17; **Builders** HM Dockyard (Chatham); **Laid down** 17 November 1960; **Launched** 5 May 1962; **Completed** January 1964; **Commissioned** 31 January 1964.

Name *Otus*; **Pennant number** S18; **Builders** Scotts; **Laid down** 31 May 1961; **Launched** 17 October 1962; **Completed** 1963; **Commissioned** 5 October 1963.

Name *Opportune*; **Pennant number** S20; **Builders** Scotts; **Laid down** 21 December 1961; **Launched** 23 May 1963; **Completed** 1964; **Commissioned** 29 December 1964.

Name *Onyx*; **Pennant number** S 21; **Builders** Cammell Laird; **Laid down** 16 November 1964; **Launched** 18 August 1966; **Completed** 1967; **Commissioned** 20 November 1967.

Other boats *Oberon* (S09) was paid off in December 1986; *Orpheus* (S11) was paid off in January 1987.

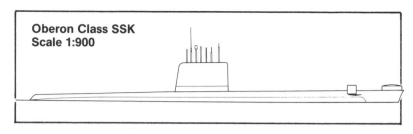

Oberon Class SSK
Scale 1:900

'Opossum' Class

Name *Opossum*; **Pennant number** S19; all details as for *Odin* except: **Sonars** 1 × 2051 (CSU 3-41) in place of 2007; **Builders** Cammell Laird; **Laid down** 21 December 1961; **Launched** 23 May 1963; **Completed** 1964; **Commissioned** 5 June 1964.

Developed from and externally identical to the early *'Porpoise'* Class SSK (conventional diesel-electric-powered submarine), the last of which were withdrawn from RN service in 1986, the *'Oberon'* Class was regarded as the world leader in the mid-1960s. By 1985, however, the boats were beginning to show their age although

Opossum *showing her new bow profile, a modification which will be fitted to other conventional submarines in due course* (Mike Lennon).

maintaining an important role in the anti-submarine forces of NATO and the Royal Navy.

SSKs are particularly quiet submarines when submerged and running on the large chloride storage batteries, which can be periodically recharged using the diesels' generators, drawing air through a snorkel/snort which is extended through the fin. During the Falklands' campaign a SSK remained on patrol for more than eighty days, bringing it to the same patrol-endurance of a larger SSN; this is a fine reflection of the ability of the boat's crew and the overall design.

'Oberon' Class boats have a multi-facet wartime role and operations might include anti-submarine and anti-surface vessel warfare, minelaying, clandestine operations (including the landing of swimmer-canoeists from the Special Boat Squadron, Royal Marines) and intelligence gathering. Because of the size and draught of the boats, they can operate closer inshore than the nuclear-powered types, and closer to enemy installations because of the quiet running afforded by electric power.

Otter was fitted with strengthened ballast tanks, twin shafts and main vents in 1984–85 to enable her to act as an underwater target for unarmed submarine weapons tests.

Opossum is the first of an important programme to fit the Type 2051 sonar to the bow, thus changing the boat's profile when surfaced. It is thought that others of the original '*Oberon*' Class will also be fitted with the system. She was also the last conventional submarine to be refitted at Chatham.

'*O*' boats are armed with conventional torpedoes of the Mk 8 and Mk 24 types, and it is possible that they may be fitted for the Marconi Underwater Systems Spearfish in due course; it is not thought that Sub-Harpoon is a weapons option for the type.

'Upholder' Class

Name *Upholder*; **Pennant number** S40; **Standard displacement** 2,000 tons; **Full displacement** 2,400 tons (dived); **Length** 70.3 m; **Beam** 7.6 m; **Draught** 5.5 m; **Propulsion** 2 × Paxman diesels, 2 × General Electric alternators, 1 × General Electric motor (5,400 hp), 1 × shaft; **Speed (surfaced)** 12 kt; **Speed (dived)** 20 kt; **Complement** 7 officers and 37 ratings; **Armament** 6 × 53 cm forward torpedo tubes; **Sensors** 1 × 1007; **Sonars** 1 × 2024 TA, 1 × 2040; **Builders** Vickers (Barrow); **Laid down** 1986; **Launched** 2 December 1986; **Completed** 1988; **Commissioned** 1989.

Although a complete class of the Vickers Type 2400 conventional submarines is planned, only three more have been indicated by

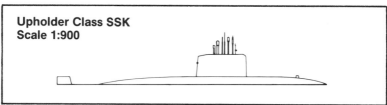

Upholder Class SSK
Scale 1:900

Top *Artist's impression of the Type 2400* (Vickers).

competitive tender at present: *Unseen* (S41), *Ursula* (S42) and *Unicorn* (S43). The design is larger than originally planned but it has an endurance of 49 days without re-supply and can transit 2,500 nm without re-fuelling.

Amongst the new systems aboard is the Type 2024 towed array sonar and the bow-mounted Type 2040; it is the first time that a modern British SSK has been driven via a single screw/shaft and for which the Paxman Valenta diesel engine has been provided (the same type as the Type 23 frigate).

Above *HMS* Ark Royal *photographed in the English Channel in July 1985.*

Below *HMS* Illustrious *photographed in June 1984.*

Above Fearless *off the Norwegian coast in March 1983.*

Below *A 'Swiftsure' Class SSN venting her tanks.*

Above *HMS* Conqueror *at speed on the surface.*

Below *HMS* Otter, *an 'Oberon' Class conventional submarine.*

Above *HMS* York, *a Type 42 Batch 3, off Spithead in July 1985.*

Below *HMS* Gloucester, *third of the* 'Manchester' *Class to enter commission.*

GUIDED MISSILE DESTROYERS
Type 82 'Bristol' Class

Name *Bristol*; **Pennant number** D23; **Flight deck code** BS; **Standard displacement** 6,100 tons; **Full displacement** 7,100 tons; **Length (overall)** 154.5 m; **Beam** 16.8 m; **Draught** 5.2 m; **Propulsion** COSAG, 2 × Standard Range steam turbines & 2 × Olympus TM1A gas turbines (30,000 shp); **Range** 5,000 nm at 18 kt; **Speed** 30 kt; **Complement** 29 officers and 367 ratings; **Armament** 1 × 114 mm Mk 8, 1 × Sea Dart GWS 30, 2 × 20 mm Oerlikon GP, 2 × 20 mm GAM-B01, 2 × 30 mm GCM (twin), Corvus; **Sensors** 2 × 909, 1 × 1022, 1 × 992Q, 1 × 1006, EW and DF, SCOT, IFF; **Sonars** 1 × 162, 1 × 182, 1 × 184, 1 × 185; **Aircraft** No facilities for embarked flight; **Builders** Swan Hunter; **Laid down** 15 November 1967; **Launched** 30 June 1969; **Completed** December 1972; **Commissioned** 31 March 1973; **Refits** 1979–80, 1984–86.

The Type 82s were designed to provide area air defence for the new class of conventional aircraft carriers being developed for the Royal Navy in the 1960s, called CVA-01. When the aircraft carriers were

Designed to operate as an aircraft carrier's consort, Bristol *is now used as a flagship. The post-Falklands close-in weapons can be easily seen amidships* (RN/FPU).

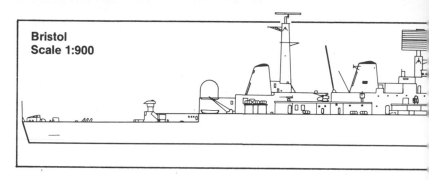

Bristol
Scale 1:900

cancelled, so were the escorts except *Bristol*. She was used as the Sea Dart trials ship in 1972, but unusually for a modern warship, especially one designated as a destroyer, the ship does not carry an embarked flight because there are no hangar facilities, only a limited flight deck.

After her 1979–80 refit, she is fully fitted to act as a command and control flagship for one of the seagoing Admirals, particularly Flag Officer Third Flotilla (FOF3), with such facilities as SCOT (Satellite Communications Onboard Terminal), the US Navy's SATCOMM WSC-3 and an intertial navigation system linked into ADAWS-2

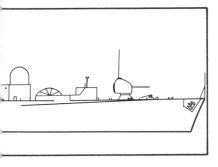

tactical information and control system. Following operations in the Falklands, *Bristol* was fitted with additional close-in weapons although the proposed fitting of Phalanx CIWS has not come about. In the next few years, Type 996 radar will replace the existing Type 992Q.

'County' Class

Name *Fife*; **Pennant number** D20; **Flight deck code** FF; **Standard displacement** 5,440 tons; **Full displacement** 6,200 tons; **Length (overall)** 158.7 m; **Beam** 16.5 m; **Draught** 6.3 m; **Propulsion** COSAG, 2 × steam

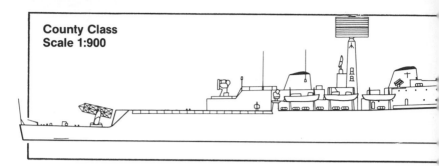

County Class
Scale 1:900

turbines (30,000 shp), 4 × gas turbines (30,000 shp), 2 × shafts; **Range** 5,000 nm at 18 kt; **Speed** 30 kt; **Complement** 33 officers and 438 ratings; **Armament** 1 × 2 114 mm Mk 6, 4 × Exocet single cell launchers, 2 × Seacat launchers; 1 × Seaslug II launcher (obsolecent), 2 × Mk 32 STWS, 3 × 20 mm Oerlikon GP, Corvus; **Sensors** 1 × 278, 1 × 965, 1 × 992R, 1 × 901, 1 × MRS 3/903, 1 × GWS 22/904, 1 × 1006, EW and DF gear, SCOT, IFF; **Sonars** 1 × 182, 1 × 184; **Aircraft** 1 × Lynx HAS 2; **Builders** Fairfield (Govan); **Laid down** 1 June 1962; **Launched** 9 July 1964; **Completed** 1966; **Commissioned** 21 June 1966; **Refits** 1970–71; 1980–83.

Glamorgan (D19) was put on the disposal list in December 1986. Previous ships of the class were *Hampshire* (paid off in 1976), *Devonshire* (expended as target in 1984), *Kent* (sold for scrap in 1985), *London* (sold to Pakistan in 1982), *Antrim* (sold to Chile in 1984) and *Norfolk* (sold to Chile in 1981).

The 'County' Class could well be regarded as light cruisers because of their original role and accommodation facilities, but because the design was built around the Seaslug medium-range, beam-riding missile system and the Seacat short-range surface-to-air missile system, they were classed as guided missile destroyers, the first in RN service. The intended role was that of area air defence escort for conventional aircraft carriers and to provide a 'police' role in the Far East.

Besides the air defence missiles and the Mk 6 dual purpose gun turrets (one was later removed on all eight in the class to be replaced by the Aerospatiale MM38 Exocet), the ships carried a Westland Wessex HAS 1 (later HAS 3) anti-submarine helicopter and in 1983, *Fife* was fitted with the Mk 32 Shipborne Torpedo Weapon System (STWS) which fires Mk 46 and Stingray torpedoes for close-in ASW defence. From 1983, both *Glamorgan* and *Fife* embarked a Lynx HAS 2 helicopter which is capable of carrying Sea Skua anti-shipping missile.

Although still capable ships, the obsolescence of the missile

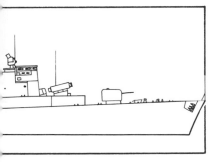

Below *Displaying her Type 909 Sea Dart radars uncovered,* Newcastle *also sports the Type 1022 radar in place of the Type 965 (RN/HMS Osprey).*

system and its vulnerability to anti-radiation missiles (following the beam-riding source) as well as the large amidships magazine, has dictated that the class will be paid off completely by 1990. In 1987, only *Fife* remains in commission.

Type 42 Batch 1, 'Birmingham' Class

Name *Birmingham*; **Pennant number** D86; **Flight deck code** BM; **Standard displacement** 3,150 tons; **Full displacement** 4,100 tons; **Length (overall)** 125.0 m; **Beam** 14.3 m; **Draught** 5.8 m; **Propulsion** COGOG, 2 × Olympus

Inset *During the South Atlantic conflict, it was shown that the 7.62 mm general purpose machine-gun was a credible defence weapon; this example is shown in* Birmingham *(Attewell Engineering).*

Background photograph Birmingham, *showing the modifications to the close-in weapons battery which have meant the removal of the ship's boats* (RN/HMS *Osprey*).

TM3B (50,000 shp) and 2 × Tyne RM1C gas turbines (9,700 shp), 2 × shafts; **Range** 4,500 nm at 18 kt; **Speed** 30 kt; **Complement** 26 officers and 273 ratings; **Armament** 1 × 114 mm Mk 8, 1 × Sea Dart GWS 30, 2 × 20 mm Oerlikon GP, 2 × 20 mm GAM-B01, 2 × 30 mm GCM (twin), 2 × Mk 32 STWS, Corvus, Mk 36 SRBOC; **Sensors** 2 × 909, 1 × 965 (1 × 1022 as refit), 1 × 992Q (1 × 996 as refit), 1 × 1006, EW & DF sets (including Abbey Hill), IFF, SCOT (for Skynet); **Sonars** 1 × 162M, 1 × 184; **Aircraft** 1 × Lynx HAS 2/3; **Builders** Cammell Laird; **Laid down** 28 March 1972; **Launched** 30 July 1973; **Completed** 1976; **Commissioned** 3 December 1976.

Name *Newcastle*; **Pennant number** D87; **Flight deck code** NC; **Complement** 21 officers and 278 ratings; **Armament** 1 × Phalanx not proceeded with; **Sensors** 1 × 1022 replaces 965; **Builders** Swan Hunter; **Laid down** 21 February 1973; **Launched** 24 April 1975; **Completed** February 1978; **Commissioned** 23 March 1978.

Name *Glasgow*; **Pennant number** D88; **Flight deck code** GW; **Complement** 21 officers and 249 ratings; **Builders** Swan Hunter; **Laid down** 7 March 1974; **Launched** 14 April 1976; **Completed** 9 March 1977; **Commissioned** 24 May 1977.

Name *Cardiff*; **Pennant number** D108; **Flight deck code** CF; **Complement** 20 officers and 260 ratings; **Sensors** 1 × 1022 replaces 965; **Builders** Vickers (Barrow); **Laid down** 3 November 1972; **Launched** 22 February 1974; **Completed** 1979; **Commissioned** 24 September 1979.

Sheffield was lost in the South Atlantic on 10 May after being hit by an Exocet missile on 4 May 1982; *Coventry* was lost in the South Atlantic on 25 May 1982 after bombing.

Type 42 Batch 2, 'Exeter' Class

Name *Exeter*; **Pennant number** D89; **Flight deck code** EX; **Sensors** 1 × 1022 at building; **Sonar** 1 × 2016 in place of 184; **Builders** Swan Hunter; **Laid down** 22 July 1976; **Launched** 25 April 1978; **Completed** 29 August 1980; **Commissioned** 19 September 1980.

Name *Southampton*; **Pennant number** D90; **Flight deck code** SN; **Builders** Vosper Thornycroft; **Laid down** 21 October 1976; **Launched** 29 January 1979; **Completed** 17 August 1981; **Commissioned** 31 October 1981.

Name *Nottingham*; **Pennant number** D91; **Flight deck code** NM; **Builders** Vosper Thornycroft; **Laid down** 6 February 1978; **Launched** 18 February 1980; **Completed** 19 November 1982; **Commissioned** 8 April 1983.

Considered a hero of the Falklands, Exeter *at sea* (RN/FPU).

Southampton *in company with* Phoebe, *a towed-array frigate* (RN/HMS *Illustrious*/LA(Phot) Harding).

Below Nottingham's *over the horizon capability is greatly enhanced by her Lynx helicopter* (RN/FPU).

Type 42 Batch 1/2
Scale 1:900

Bottom *Although fitted with Mk32 STWS, Liverpool is pictured prior to being fitted with the new CIWS battery* (RN).

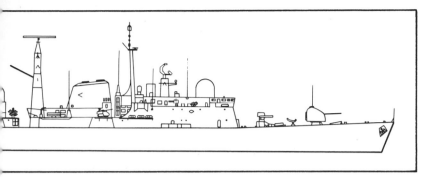

Name *Liverpool*; **Pennant number** D92; **Flight deck code** LP; **Builders** Cammell Laird; **Laid down** 5 July 1978; **Launched** 25 September 1980; **Completed** 12 May 1982; **Commissioned** 9 July 1982.

The first British destroyers to be built with gas turbine propulsion, using Rolls-Royce marinized turbines, Tynes for cruising and Olympus for full power which can be reached in about thirty seconds. The ships need only about 75 per cent of the marine engineering staff of warships of similar size. The ships' role is area air defence, although the lack of quick-reaction surface-to-air missiles, like Seawolf, was shown in the Falklands' conflict when the original name ship of the class *Sheffield*, and *Coventry* were lost. It is thought that Vertical Launch Seawolf is being studied for eventual refit to the class. After returning from Operation 'Corporate', all Type 42s then in commission were fitted with extra close-in weapons.

The only significant differences between the four Batch 1 destroyers in this class and the four Batch 2 ships is that the latter were built with Type 1022 radar, rather than the Type 965 AKE-2. There were some additional changes to the operations room fit and the data processing facilities.

The ships are highly manoeuvrable, stable and can provide very adequate air defence with Sea Dart GWS 30, which system is likely to be updated by the replacement of the Type 992Q target acquisition radar with the new Plessey Type 996. It is understood that until 1981 it was proposed to update Sea Dart to GWS 31 standard using the Type 1030 radar, but from 1987 the existing Sea Dart warheads will be enhanced.

The air defence facilities aboard the ships including the computer-enhanced Action Data Automated Weapons System (ADAWS) 4 (in the Batch 1 ships) and the more advanced ADAWS 7, using two Ferranti FM 1600 computers and data links (in the Batch 2 ships)

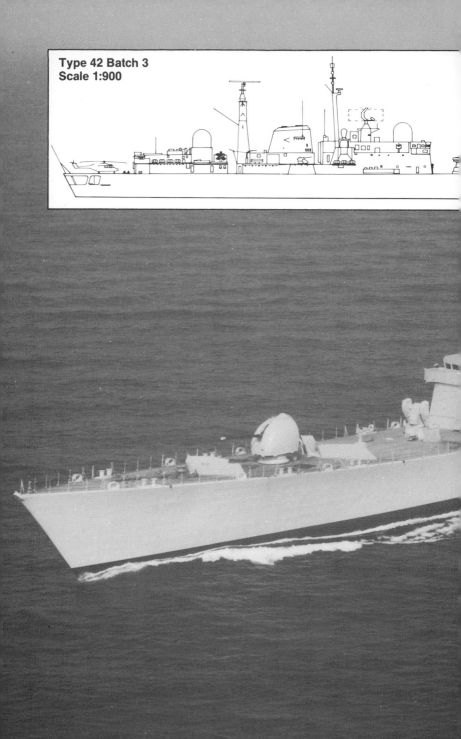

Type 42 Batch 3
Scale 1:900

Manchester, *the first of the stretched Type 42 destroyers, shows her extended hull* (RN/FPU).

which also provide weapon direction facilities for the Vickers Mk 8 gun and the Sea Dart system.

The ships' embarked helicopter is equipped to carry Mk 44, Mk 46 and Stingray anti-submarine torpedoes, Mk 11 depth bombs and the British Aerospace Sea Skua anti-shipping missile. The Westland Lynx is fitted with Ferranti Sea Spray radar and Racal Orange Crop ESM.

Type 42 Batch 3, 'Manchester' Class

Name *Manchester*; **Pennant number** D95; **Flight deck code** MC; **Standard displacement** 4,100 tons; **Full displacement** 5,350 tons; **Length (overall)** 141.1 m; **Beam** 14.9 m; **Draught** 5.8 m; **Propulsion** As for Batch 1; **Range** As for Batch 1; **Complement** 26 officers and 275 ratings; **Armament** As for Batch 1; **Sensors** As for Batch 2 (with Type 996 as refit); **Sonars** As for Batch 2; **Aircraft** 1 × Lynx HAS 3; **Builders** Vickers (Barrow); **Laid down** 19 May 1978; **Launched** 24 November 1980; **Completed** 19 November 1982; **Commissioned** 16 December 1982.

Name *Gloucester*; **Pennant number** D96; **Flight deck code** GC; **Builders** Vosper Thornycroft; **Laid down** 29 October 1979; **Launched** 2 November 1982; **Completed** November 1984; **Commissioned** 11 September 1985.

Name *Edinburgh*; **Pennant number** D97; **Flight deck code** EB; **Sensors** 1 × 996 in place of 992; **Builders** Cammell Laird; **Laid down** 8 September 1980; **Launched** 17 April 1983; **Completed** 20 July 1985; **Commissioned** 17 December 1985.

Name *York*; **Pennant number** D98; **Flight deck code** YK; **Sensors** 1 × 996; **Builders** Swan Hunter; **Laid down** 18 January 1980; **Launched** 21 June 1982; **Completed** 25 March 1985; **Commissioned** 9 August 1985.

As a result of the experience gained with the first Type 42 guided missile destroyers, it was decided to stretch the design to improve seakeeping and fuel economy. In addition, the later ships were completed after some internal modification arising from action in the South Atlantic in 1982 had been incorporated.

The fitting of the improved Type 996 radar will provide better surveillance and target indication facilities and it is thought that the improved Sea Dart missile will be carried by the class. Despite comments in the 1981 Defence Review that these ships will not have a half-life refit, it is thought that the Vertical Launch Seawolf system will be ordered for at least the Batch 3 destroyers in due course. It is also possible that Goalkeeper CIWS could be fitted but another option is to fit Phalanx equipment taken from '*Invincible*' Class CVSs when they receive Goalkeeper in due course.

FRIGATES

Type 12 (Modified) 'Rothesay' Class

Name *Rothesay*; **Pennant number** F107; **Flight deck code** RO; **Standard displacement** 2,380 tons; **Full displacement** 2,800 tons; **Length (overall)** 109.7 m; **Beam** 12.5 m; **Draught** 5.3 m; **Propulsion** 2 × Admiralty Standard Range turbines (15,000 shp each), 2 × shafts; **Range** 4,200 nm at 12 kt; **Speed** 30 kt; **Complement** 15 officers and 220 ratings; **Armament** 1 × 2 114 mm Mk 6, 2 × 20 mm Oerlikon GP, 1 × Seacat launcher, 1 × Limbo Mk 10, 2 × Corvus; **Sensors** 1 × 975, 1 × 994, 1 × GWS 22/903, Direction finding; **Sonars** 1 × 170; 1 × 177; **Aircraft** 1 × Wasp HAS 1; **Builders** Yarrow; **Laid**

Although rather long in the tooth now, the 'Rothesay' *Class have been very useful frigates; this is* Rothesay *herself preparing to replenish at Sea* (RN).

Clean lines but obsolescent sensors in Berwick (RN).

down 6 November 1956; **Launched** 9 December 1957; **Completed** 1959; **Commissioned** 23 April 1960; Seacat modernization 1966–68; **Refit** 1984–85.

Name *Plymouth*; **Pennant number** F126; **Flight deck code** PL; **Builders** HM Dockyard (Plymouth); **Laid down** 1 July 1958; **Launched** 20 July 1959; **Completed** 1961; **Commissioned** 11 May 1961; Seacat modernization 1969–71; **Refit** 1985–86.

Others in class *Yarmouth* (paid off on 24 April 1986); *Falmouth* (paid off in December 1984); *Brighton* (paid off in 1984); *Lowestoft* (converted to trials ship, paid off on 31 March 1985, sunk as target 1986); *Londonderry* (converted to trials ship in 1975–79 and paid off); *Rhyl* (paid off in 1985); *Berwick* paid off to the Standby Squadron in 1986.

Designed as specialist anti-submarine frigates, based on the earlier Type 12 '*Whitby*' Class, the last of which, *Torquay*, was paid off in 1985, the '*Rothesay*' Class is destined to remain in service until 1988 when both the hulls will have reached the end of their useful lives and the embarked helicopter, the Wasp, will have been phased out of service. The ships are expensive to man and run.

Between 1966–70, the class was modified to carry Seacat surface-to-air guided missiles, which also have a limited surface-to-surface role, and the 40 mm Bofors mountings were landed. Originally, two

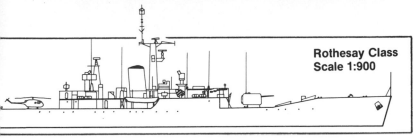

Rothesay Class
Scale 1:900

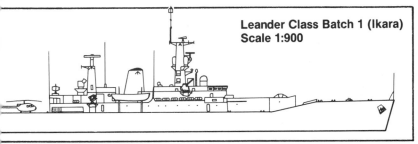

Leander Class Batch 1 (Ikara)
Scale 1:900

sets of the Mk 10 ASW mortar were carried but one set was removed to allow for a flight deck. The class played an important role in the development of the modern British frigate and were the prototypes for the later '*Leander*' Class.

As a result of the Falklands' conflict, when deployed to the South Atlantic for the Falkland Islands' peace patrol, ships of the class have been fitted with up to 4 × GAM-B01 guns.

Type 12 (Improved) 'Leander' Class

Batch 1: Ikara 'Leander'

Name *Aurora*; **Pennant number** F10; **Flight deck code** AU; **Standard displacement** 2,450 tons; **Full displacement** 2,860 tons; **Length (overall)** 113.5 m; **Beam** 12.5 m; **Draught** 5.5 m; **Propulsion** 2 × reduction geared steam turbines (30,000 shp), 2 × shafts; **Range** 4,000 nm at 15 kt; **Speed** 28 kt; **Complement** 20 officers and 237 ratings; **Armament** 1 × Ikara system, 2 × 40 mm Bofors GP Mk 9, 2 × Seacat launchers, 1 × Limbo Mk 10, 2 × Corvus; **Sensors** 1 × 975, 1 × 992, 1 × 993, SCOT, EW, IFF, DF; **Sonars** 1 × 170, 1 × 184, 1 × 199 VDS; **Aircraft** 1 × Wasp HAS 1; **Builders** John Brown; **Laid down** 1 June 1961; **Launched** 28 November 1962; **Completed** 1964; **Commissioned** 9 April 1964; Ikara modernization 1973–75; **Refit** 1984–85.

Name *Euryalus*; **Pennant number** F15; **Flight deck code** EU; **Builders** Scotts; **Laid down** 2 November 1961; **Launched** 6 June 1963; **Completed** 1964; **Commissioned** 16 September 1964; Ikara modernization 1974–76.

Aurora, preparing to take on fuel, is one of the few frigates with the variable depth sonar (right aft) (RN/FPU).

Name *Arethusa*; **Pennant number** F38; **Flight deck code** AR; **Builders** Whites; **Laid down** 7 September 1962; **Launched** 5 November 1963; **Completed** 1965; **Commissioned** 24 November 1965; Ikara modernization 1975-77.

Name *Naiad*; **Pennant number** F39; **Flight deck code** NA; **Complement** 17 officers and 239 ratings; **Builders** Yarrow; **Laid down** 30 October 1962; **Launched** 4 November 1963; **Completed** 1965; **Commissioned** 15 March 1965; Ikara modernization 1972-75.

The *'Leanders'* are undoubtedly the outstanding frigates of the postwar period and were built in greater numbers than any other major British surface combat ship. Not only has the class been highly successful in the Royal Navy but there has been considerable foreign naval interest in the design. The design role was officially classed as 'general purpose' but the bulk of the systems have been developed to give good ASW abilities. By early 1986, the class was beginning to show its age, both in terms of obsolescent systems and high-cost manning. As the new Type 22 destroyers enter service, *'Leanders'* are paid off, some for disposal by scrapping, others for sale to friendly navies.

The design can be traced to the *'Whitby'* Class but unlike other Type 12s, the *'Leanders'* were designed to operate helicopters, to be armed with guided missiles and to have long-range search radar installed. Over a dozen shipyards were involved in the building of the

Euryalus, *being put through her paces for the camera off Portland, shows the Ikara missile on its launcher, forward of the bridge. Note also the Mk 10 mortar well* (RN/PFU).

class and during its evolution several changes were made, including the re-arrangement of the internal accommodation, uprating of the steam turbines and, in the case of the Batch 3 ships, the physical dimensions were altered (see below).

Some ships have had the Type 199 Variable Depth Sonar (VDS) removed and the well plated over for extra accommodation, especially for the embarked Royal Marines detachment. All the Batch 1 '*Leanders*' have been converted to carry the Anglo-Australian medium range guided anti-submarine weapon system, Ikara.

Leander (F109) was originally named *Weymouth*, and paid off in 1986; *Penelope* (F127) was laid down as *Coventry*; *Dido*, ex-*Hastings* (F104), was paid off into Royal New Zealand Naval service in July 1983 as *Southland*; *Ajax* (F114) paid off in 1985; and *Galatea* (F18) paid off in 1986.

Batch 2: Exocet 'Leander'

Name *Minerva*; **Pennant number** F45; **Flight deck code** MV; **Standard displacement** As Batch 1; **Full displacement** 3,200 tons; **Length and Beam** as Batch 1; **Draught** 5.8 m; **Armament** 4 × Exocet single cell launchers, 3 × Seacat launchers, 2 × 40 mm Bofors GP Mk9, 2 × Mk 32 STWS-1, 2 × Corvus; **Sensors** 1 × 965; 1 × 975, 1 × 993, 2 × GWS 22, SCOT, IFF, EW, DF; **Sonar** 1 × 184; **Aircraft** 1 × Lynx HAS 2/3; **Builders** Vickers; **Laid down** 25 July 1963; **Launched** 19 December 1964; **Completed** 1967; **Commissioned** 7 September 1967; Exocet modernization 1976-79; **Refit** 1982-83.

Danae *is a Batch 2* 'Leander' *which has seen considerable service in the South Atlantic*

Name *Danae*; **Pennant number** F47; **Flight deck code** DN; **Complement** 18 officers and 205 ratings; **Builders** HM Dockyard (Devonport); **Laid down** 16 December 1964; **Launched** 31 October 1965; **Completed** September 1967; **Commissioned** 7 September 1967; Exocet modernization 1977–78.

Name *Penelope*; **Pennant number** F127; **Flight deck code** PE; **Complement** 19 officers and 200 ratings; **Builders** Vickers; **Laid down** 14 March 1961; **Launched** 17 August 1962; **Completed** 1963; **Commissioned** 31 October 1963; Seawolf trials refit 1971–73; Exocet modernization 1980–82.

Name *Juno*; **Pennant number** F52; **Flight deck code** JO; **Complement** 18 officers and 210 ratings; **Builders** Thornycroft; **Laid down** 27 November 1964; **Launched** 8 February 1966; **Completed** 1967; **Commissioned** 17 August 1967; **Refit** 1981–82; Training ship conversion 1984–85.

With the increasing need to provide surface escorts, particularly those which might operate alone in times of tension, with a viable over-the-horizon anti-ship weapons system, the Royal Navy turned to the French Aerospatiale company and purchased the MM38 Exocet anti-ship guided missile. After a conversion at Naval dockyards, which involved the removal of the Mk 6 mounting, four single-cell Exocet launchers were installed forward of the bridge.

In addition, a third Seacat surface-to-air missile launcher was installed forward of the Exocets, on the breakwater, presumably to provide air defence when the ship was heading towards a threat to be engaged with Exocet. The anti-ship missile has a limited firing envelope and the after Seacat mountings would be out of launch constraints.

In 1982, following the Falklands' conflict, *Juno's* conversion to Exocet standard at Rosyth was abandoned and the ship replaced *Torquay*, the last of the Type 12 '*Whitby*' Class frigates, as the Fleet Training Ship in April 1985.

Star of a television series, Phoebe *continues to be an important asset in the anti-submarine war in her towed array role* (RN/FPU).

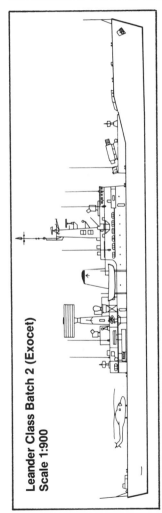

Leander Class Batch 2 (Exocet)
Scale 1:900

Argonaut *is a towed array 'Leander', armed with the MM38 Exocet missile system* (RN/FPU).

Batch 2: Towed Array 'Leander'

Name *Cleopatra*; **Pennant number** F28; **Flight deck code** CP; **Standard displacement** 2,450 tons; **Full displacement** 3,200 tons; **Length, Beam and Draught** As Batch 2; **Complement** 20 officers and 230 ratings; **Armament** 4 × Exocet single-cell launchers, 2 × Seacat launchers, 2 × 20 mm Oerlikon GP, 2 × Mk 32 STWS-1, 2 × Corvus, 1 × SRBOC; **Sensors** 1 × 975, 1 × 993, 1 × GWS 22, SCOT, IFF, EW, DF; **Sonars** 1 × 184, 1 × 2031 (towed array); **Aircraft** 1 × Lynx HAS 2/3 (when embarked); **Builders** HM Dockyard (Devonport); **Laid down** 19 June 1963; **Launched** 25 March 1964; **Completed** December 1965; **Commissioned** 1 March 1966; Exocet modernization 1972–75.

Name *Sirius*; **Pennant number** F40; **Flight deck code** SS; **Complement** 20 officers and 203 ratings; **Builders** HM Dockyard (Portsmouth); **Laid down** 9 August 1963; **Launched** 22 September 1964; **Completed** May 1966; **Commissioned** 15 June 1966; Exocet modernization 1975–77.

Name *Phoebe*; **Pennant number** F42; **Flight deck code** PB; **Complement** 20 officers and 230 ratings; **Builders** Alex Stephens; **Laid down** 3 June 1963; **Launched** 8 July 1964; **Completed** 1966; **Commissioned** 14 April 1966; Exocet modernization 1974–77.

Name *Argonaut*; **Pennant number** F56; **Flight deck code** AT; **Complement** 18 officers and 206 ratings; **Builders** Hawthorn Leslie; **Laid down** 27 November 1964; **Launched** 8 February 1966; **Completed** 1967; **Commissioned** 17 August 1966; Exocet modernization 1978–80.

This batch of four frigates has been modified for specialist anti-submarine work with the fitting of the Plessey Marine Type 2031 towed-array system on the starboard quarterdeck. To save top-weight, the forward Seacat launcher has been removed, the Exocet mountings lowered, the seaboats replaced by Pacific 22 'seariders', the 40 mm Bofors replaced by 20 mm Oerlikon GP Mk 9 guns, the Mk 32 STWS-1 has been removed to the main deck and the Type 965 radar has been landed in favour of a Type 994 air/surface warning set. The hull-mounted Type 184 sonar has been retained.

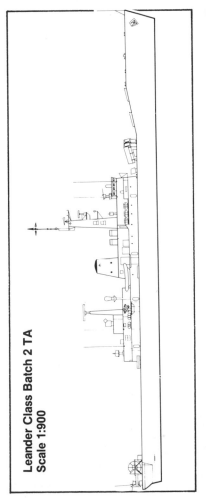

Leander Class Batch 2 TA
Scale 1:900

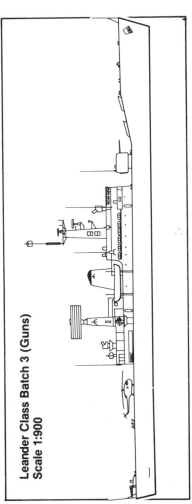

Leander Class Batch 3 (Guns)
Scale 1:900

Batch 3: Broad-beamed 'Leander'

Name *Achilles*; **Pennant number** F12; **Flight deck code** AC; **Standard displacement** 2,500 tons; **Full displacement** 2,962 tons; **Length** As Batch 1; **Beam** 13.1 m; **Draught** As Batch 1; **Complement** 17 officers and 243 ratings; **Armament** 1 × 2 114 mm Mk 6, 2 × 20 mm Oerlikon GP, 1 × 20 mm Oerlikon GAM-B01 (flt deck), 1 × Seacat launcher, 1 × Limbo Mk 10, 2 × Corvus; **Sensors** 1 × 965, 1 × 975, 1 × 993, IFF, DF, EW, GWS 22/MRS 3; **Sonar** 1 × 184; **Builders** Yarrow; **Laid down** 1 December 1967; **Launched** 21 November 1968; **Completed** 1970; **Commissioned** 9 July 1970.

Name *Diomede*; **Pennant number** F16; **Flight deck code** DM; **Laid down** 30 January 1968; **Launched** 15 April 1969; **Completed** 1971; **Commissioned** 2 April 1971.

Name *Apollo*; **Pennant number** F70; **Flight deck code** AP; **Laid down** 1 May 1969; **Launched** 15 October 1970; **Completed** May 1972; **Commissioned** 28 May 1972.

Name *Ariadne*; **Pennant number** F72; **Flight deck code** AE; **Complement** 20 officers and 240 ratings; **Laid down** 1 November 1969; **Launched** 10 September 1971; **Completed** 1972; **Commissioned** 10 February 1973.

Baccante (F69) paid off to Royal New Zealand Navy in October 1982.

Apollo is one of the remaining 'Gun Leanders' *in service, carrying the Mk6 114 mm gun* (RN/FPU).

Designed and refitted to carry both Seawolf (six cell launcher) and Exocet, Charybdis *is a Batch 3* 'Leander' (RN/HMS *Osprey*).

All built by Yarrow, the last four broad-beamed *'Leanders'* have a reputation for better seakeeping and cruise economy, but are basically the same ships in terms of role. These four ships have not received Seawolf, retain the 144 mm gun mounting and could not be modernized as a result of the far-reaching 1981 Defence White Paper.

Batch 3: Seawolf 'Leander'

Name *Andromeda*; **Pennant number** F57; **Flight deck code** AM; **Standard displacement** As Batch 3; **Full displacement** 3,200 tons; **Length, Beam and Draught** As Batch 3; **Complement** 35 officers and 226 ratings; **Armament** 4 × Exocet single-cell launchers, 1 × 6 Seawolf Point Defence Missile System, 2 × Mk 32 STWS-1, 2 × 20 mm Oerlikon GP, 2 × Corvus; **Sensors** 1 × 910, 1 × 967, 1 × 1006, EW, DF, SCOT, IFF; **Sonar** 1 × 2016; **Aircraft** 1 × Lynx HAS 2/3; **Builders** HM Dockyard (Portsmouth); **Laid down** 25 May 1966; **Launched** 24 May 1967; **Completed** 1968; **Commissioned** 2 December 1968; Exocet modernization 1977–81; Refit 1985–86.

Alongside at Gibraltar, Jupiter *and a sister ship both wear an '8' on the funnel to show they are members of the Eighth Frigate Squadron* (RN/HMS *Illustrious*/LA(Phot) Harding).

Name *Hermione*; **Pennant number** F58, **Flight deck code** HM; **Complement** 18 officers and 196 ratings; **Builders** Alex Stephens; **Laid down** 6 December 1965; **Launched** 26 April 1967; **Completed** 1969; **Commissioned** 11 July 1969; Exocet modernization 1980–82.

Name *Jupiter*; **Pennant number** F60; **Flight deck code** JP; **Complement** As *Hermione*; **Builders** Yarrow; **Laid down** 3 October 1966; **Launched** 4 September 1967; **Completed** 1969; **Commissioned** 9 August 1969; Exocet modernization 1980–83.

Name *Scylla*; **Pennant number** F71; **Flight deck code** SC; **Complement** As *Hermione*; **Builders** HM Dockyard (Devonport); **Laid down** 17 May 1967; **Launched** 8 August 1968; **Completed** 12 February 1970; **Commissioned** 14 February 1970; Exocet modernization 1980–85.

Name *Charybdis*; **Pennant number** F75; **Flight deck code** CS; **Builders** Harland & Wolff; **Laid down** 27 January 1967; **Launched** 28 February 1968; **Completed** 1969; **Commissioned** 2 June 1969; Exocet modernization 1979–82.

In the late 1970s it was decided to refit the Batch 3 frigates, which had been built at different yards, to take both Exocet anti-ship missiles and the new British Aerospace Seawolf GWS 25 PDMS (point defence missile system). This conversion, which included the removal of the Seacat SAM launcher system and the Mk 10 Limbo mortar, cost about £70 million and as a result of the 1981 Defence White Paper work was terminated after five ships had been reworked by HM Dockyard (Devonport).

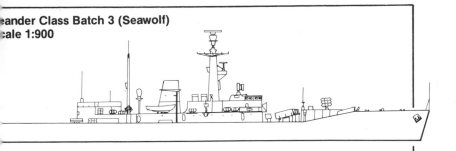

Other modifications include provision for the Westland Lynx HAS 2/3 shipborne helicopter which itself is capable of carrying the Mk 44, Mk 46 and Stingray anti-submarine torpedoes (also fitted to the new Mk 32 STWS fitted during the refits), British Aerospace Sea Skua anti-shipping missile, the Mk 11 depth bomb and nuclear depth charges. The ships' flight decks were modified to take the helicopter's Fairey Hydraulics Harpoon deck retention system which enables the Lynx to remain on deck safely and manoeuvre in foul weather; there is also a haul-in system for the hangar party to bring the helicopter in during really bad weather conditions.

The ships' appearance was changed with the landing of the Type 965 'bedstead' radar, the re-built flat-top funnel and a new mainmast with EW suite. Below decks, the accommodation has been improved and the Operations Room has been remodelled to take extensive computerization, using the Ferranti FM 1600 system linked to the DBA 5 Computer Assisted Action Information System, interfaced with the Seawolf and the Type 2016 hull-mounted sonar.

For service in the South Atlantic, several ships have been fitted with additional 20 mm Oerlikon weapons. *Hermione* undertook trials with the Type 165 towed array sonar immediately after refit but this was removed and her ship's flight returned. *Scylla's* half-life conversion was stopped during the Falklands' conflict in order that spares from the ship could be made available to others of the class in commission.

Type 21 'Amazon' Class

Name *Amazon*; **Pennant number** F169; **Flight deck code** AZ; **Standard displacement** 2,750 tons; **Full displacement** 3,250 tons; **Length (overall)** 117.0 m; **Beam** 12.7 m; **Draught** 6.8 m; **Propulsion** COGOG 2 × Rolls-Royce Olympus TM3B (50,000 shp), 2 × RR Tyne RM1C (9,700 shp) gas turbines, 2 × shafts; **Range** 1,200 nm at 30 kt, 4,500 nm at 18 kt; **Speed** 34 kt;

Complement 11 officers and 159 ratings; **Armament** 1 × 114 mm Vickers Mk 8; 4 × Exocet GWS 50 single-cell launchers, 4 × 20 mm Oerlikon GP, 1 × Seacat GWS 24 launcher, 2 × Mk 32 STWS-1, 2 × Corvus; **Sensors** 1 × 1006, 1 × 992Q, 1 × 912/WSA 4, Cossor Mk 10 IFF, Abbey Hill UAA-1 EW; **Sonars** 1 × 162, 1 × 184M, **Aircraft** 1 × Lynx HAS 2/3 (which replaced Wasp HAS 1); **Builders** Vosper Thornycroft; **Laid down** 6 November 1969; **Launched** 26 April 1971; **Completed** 1974; **Commissioned** 11 May 1974.

Name *Active*; **Pennant number** F171; **Flight deck code** AV; **Complement** 11 officers and 160 ratings; **Builders** Vosper Thornycroft; **Laid down** 23 July 1971; **Launched** 23 November 1972; **Completed** 1977; **Commissioned** 17 June 1977.

Name *Ambuscade*; **Pennant number** F172; **Flight deck code** AB; **Complement** 12 officers and 168 ratings; **Builders** Yarrow; **Laid down** 1 September 1971; **Launched** 18 January 1973; **Completed** 1975; **Commissioned** 5 September 1975.

Name *Arrow*; **Pennant number** F173; **Flight deck code** AW; **Complement** 13 officers and 167 ratings; **Builders** Yarrow; **Laid down** 28 September 1972; **Launched** 5 February 1974; **Completed** 1976; **Commissioned** 29 July 1976.

Name *Alacrity*; **Pennant number** F174; **Flight deck code** AL; **Complement** 11 officers and 160 ratings; **Builders** Yarrow; **Laid down** 5 March 1973; **Launched** 18 September 1974; **Completed** 1977; **Commissioned** 2 July 1977.

Name *Avenger*; **Pennant number** F185; **Flight deck code** AG; **Complement** 13 officers and 160 ratings; **Builders** Yarrow; **Laid down** 30 October 1974; **Launched** 20 November 1975; **Completed** 1978; **Commissioned** 4 May 1978.

Others in class *Antelope* (F170) was lost in the South Atlantic on 24 May 1982 and *Ardent* (F184) on 21 May 1982, both to Argentine air attacks.

The Type 21 frigate is one of the most exciting designs to come from British Naval builders since 1945 for, not only is it the first to be ordered from a purely commercial design, but is the first to be designed from the keel up as gas turbine-powered. The initial design, was, however, criticized for its lack of armament and from 1976, Exocet systems were fitted to seven of the original eight in the class; *Ambuscade* was fitted in 1984–85.

The original concept to fit Seawolf PDMS was abandoned and the lack of a comprehensive air defence system was discovered during

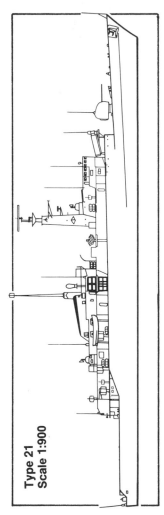

Type 21
Scale 1:900

One of the members of Global 86, the Royal Naval deployment around the world, Amazon is armed with the Mk8 gun and Exocet anti-ship missiles (RN).

Operation 'Corporate' in 1982; as a result additional 20 mm Oerlikon guns have been fitted. It is not thought that any additional systems will be fitted and no half-life modernization is expected.

The Action Information Organization in the ships was designed

Above left *Sailing past the Rock of Gibraltar,* Active *shows her clean lines resulting from a commercial design programme* (RN/FPU).

Left Ambuscade *was the last Type 21 to receive Exocet* (Paul Beaver).

Above *Operating within a task group,* Alacrity *moves alongside* Illustrious (RN/PO(Phot) du Feu).

around the DBA 2 Computer Assisted Action Information System, providing weapons control for the Seacat and Mk 8 gun mounting. It is based on the Ferranti FM 1600 computer.

The first three ships in the class (including *Antelope*) were built by the designers, Vosper Thornycroft, but the last five (including *Ardent*) were built at Yarrow's yard on the Clyde. *Active* took five years to complete as a result of component delays, especially with the Aerospatiale Exocet missile system, the ship being alongside at Southampton docks for some time; she was eventually the fifth Type 21 to be commissioned.

As a result of the Falklands' conflict, fears were expressed about the high level of aluminium in the class' superstructure and upper works; the Royal Navy is reportedly not so concerned and has indicated that the design continues to be safe and reliable.

Type 22 Batch 1: 'Broadsword' Class

Name *Broadsword*; **Pennant number** F88; **Flight deck code** BW; **Standard displacement** 3,500 tons; **Full displacement** 4,200 tons; **Length (overall)** 131.2 m; **Beam** 14.75 m; **Draught** 4.3 m; **Propulsion** COGOG 2 × Rolls-Royce Olympus TM3B (50,000 shp), 2 × RR Tyne RM1C (9,700 shp) gas turbines, 2 × shafts; **Range** 4,500 nm at 18 kt; **Speed** 30 kt; **Complement** 25 officers and 225 ratings; **Armament** 2 × 40 mm Bofors GP Mk 9, 2 × 20 mm Oerlikon GAM-B01 (for South Atlantic), 2 × 6 Seawolf GWS 25 PDMS, 4 × Exocet GWS 50 single-cell launcher, 2 × Mk 32 STWS-1, 2 × Corvus; **Sensors** 2 × 910, 1 × 967, 1 × 968, 1 × 1006, DF, UAA–01 EW, SCOT, IFF; **Sonars** 1 × 2008, 1 × 2050; **Aircraft** 2 × Lynx HAS 3 (one carried normally); **Builders** Yarrow; **Laid down** 7 February 1975; **Launched** 12 May 1976; **Completed** 1978; **Commissioned** 4 May 1979.

Name *Battleaxe*; **Pennant number** F89; **Flight deck code** BX; **Complement** 20 officers and 203 ratings; **Laid down** 4 February 1976; **Launched** 18 May 1977; **Completed** 1980; **Commissioned** 28 March 1980.

Name *Brilliant*; **Pennant number** F90; **Flight deck code** BT; **Complement** 18 officers and 205 ratings; **Laid down** 25 March 1977; **Launched** 15 December 1978; **Completed** 10 April 1981; **Commissioned** 15 May 1981.

Broadsword has a characteristic funnel design which makes her easy to identify when not carrying pennant numbers (RN/HMS *Osprey*).

Above Danae *at sea in June 1984.*
Below Naiad *at the moment of launching an Ikara.*

Above Jupiter, *a Batch 3 Seawolf 'Leander'.*

Below Arrow, *a Type 21 frigate.*

Above *The author's namesake,* HMS Beaver *at sea* (Yarrow).

Below Ledbury, *a 'Hunt' Class MCMV* (Vosper Thornycroft).

Above Bronington, *a 'Ton' Class minehunter.*

Below *The Offshore Patrol Vessel* Leeds Castle.

Brilliant *at Portsmouth; the tall structure behind is* Dolphin's *submarine escape training tower* (RN).

Name *Brazen*; **Pennant number** F91; **Flight deck code** BZ; **Complement** 18 officers and 206 ratings; **Aircraft** 2 × Lynx HAS 3; **Laid down** 18 August 1978; **Launched** 4 March 1980; **Completed** 15 June 1982; **Commissioned** 2 July 1982.

Originally designed to be the successor to the *'Leander'* Class, the Type 22 frigates are large anti-submarine warfare escorts and initially were without gun armament. The 40 mm Bofors was added for policing duties and local air defence, but as a result of the Falklands' conflict, the Batch 3 frigates will also be fitted with the Mk 8 gun for naval gunfire support (NGS).

Built to metric standards, the ships are the first to be designed to fit the Seawolf PDMS and to carry two Lynx helicopters for anti-submarine and anti-surface vessel warfare. During the Falklands' conflict *Brilliant* became the first warship to fire Seawolf, destroying two Argentine Skyhawk jets in San Carlos water on 12 May 1982; the system malfunctioned minutes later when the second wave attacked but *Brilliant* was not damaged.

Brazen was Prince Andrew's ship until 1986 and is pictured here during patrol duties in the Arabian Gulf prior to her illustrious helicopter pilot's arrival on board (RN/FPU).

Batch 2: 'Boxer' Class

Name *Boxer*; **Pennant number** F92; **Flight deck code** BR; **Standard displacement** 4,100 tons; **Full displacement** 4,800 tons; **Length (overall)** 143.6 m; **Beam** As Batch 1; **Draught** 6.4 m; **Propulsion** As Batch 1; **Range and Speed** As Batch 1; **Complement** 30 officers and 260 ratings; **Armament** As Batch 1; **Sensors** As Batch 1; **Sonars** As Batch 1, except 1 × 2031 TA; **Builders** Yarrow; **Laid down** 1 November 1979; **Launched** 17 June 1981; **Completed** 23 September 1983; **Commissioned** 22 December 1983.

Name *Beaver*; **Pennant number** F93; **Flight deck code** BV; **Laid down** 20 June 1980; **Launched** 8 May 1982; **Completed** 1984; **Commissioned** 13 December 1984.

Name *Brave*; **Pennant number** F94; **Flight deck code** BE; **Propulsion** COGOG, 4 × Rolls-Royce Spey SM1A (37,450 shp); **Armament** As *Boxer* except Lightweight Seawolf installed; **Sensors** As Batch 1, except 2 × Marconi 805 Seawolf control and 1 × 967M; **Aircraft** 2 × Lynx HAS 3/Sea King HAS 5/EH 101; **Laid down** 24 May 1982; **Launched** 19 November 1983; **Completed** 21 February 1986; **Commissioned** 4 July 1986.

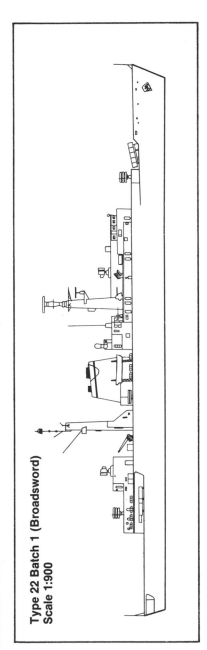

Type 22 Batch 1 (Broadsword)
Scale 1:900

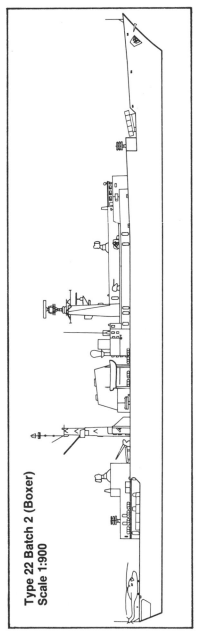

Type 22 Batch 2 (Boxer)
Scale 1:900

Name *London* (ex-*Bloodhound*); **Pennant number** F95; **Flight deck code** LN; **Propulsion** COGAG, 2 × Rolls-Royce Spey SM1A (37,540 shp), 2 × RR Tyne TM1C (9,700 shp), 2 × shafts; **Laid down** 7 February 1983; **Launched** 27 October 1984; **Completed** 1986; **Commissioned** 1987.

Name *Sheffield*; **Pennant number** F96; **Flight deck code** SD; **Builders** Swan Hunter; **Laid down** 29 March 1984; **Launched** March 1986; **Completed** 1987; **Commissioned** 1988.

Name *Coventry*; **Pennant number** F96; **Flight deck code** CV; **Builders** Swan Hunter (Wallsend); **Laid down** 29 March 1984; **Launched** 8 April 1986; **Completed** 1987; **Commissioned** 1988.

The Type 22 Batch 2 frigate has been stretched and remodelled internally as a result of the trials carried out in the earlier Batch 1 ships. In addition, the Type 2031 towed-array sonar (TA) has been added to all six ships.

From *Brave* onwards, the flight deck and hangar arrangements

Boxer was the first of the stretched Type 22 frigates and has a primary role of anti-submarine warfare (RN/PFU).

The first frigate to be complemented with two Lynx HAS 2 helicopters, Beaver *was winner of the 1985 Boyd Trophy and a member of Global 86 deployment* (RN/HMS *Osprey*).

have been altered to embark the Sea King HAS 5 (or Mk 6 if it is ordered) and eventually the EH 101 anti-submarine helicopter. In addition, *Brave* has been fitted with four Rolls-Royce Spey gas turbines; the last three in the Batch having the COGAG arrangement of Spey and Tyne. This combination of propulsion gives better fuel economy.

Boxer carried out the initial trials with the CACS 2 (Computer Assisted Command System) which was developed in the early 1980s to replace the existing ADAWS and CAAIS systems. It uses the high technology Ferranti FM1600E computer and the Admiralty Surface Weapons Establishment serial highway (ASH) to pass information around the ship with ease. The ships are also fitted with NATO Data Link 11 and 14 for the passing of secure information.

When the ships are deployed to the Arabian Sea or the South Atlantic, they carry additional 20 mm Oerlikon GAM-B01 gun mountings for close-in defence. The Batch 2 frigates may be fitted with Goalkeeper CIWS in due course.

Batch 3: 'Cornwall' Class

Name *Cornwall*; **Pennant number** F99; **Flight deck code** CW; **Standard displacement** 4,200 tons; **Full displacement** 4,900 tons; **Length, Beam and Draught** As Batch 2; **Propulsion, Range and Speed** As *London*; **Complement** 31 officers and 259 ratings; **Armament** 1 × 114 mm Vickers Mk8, 2 × 30 mm Goalkeeper, 2 × 6 Lightweight Seawolf launchers, 8 × Harpoon single cell launchers, 2 × Corvus CM, 2 × SRBOC CM, 2 × Mk 32 STWS-2; **Sensors** As *Brave*, except 1 × 996 to replace 967/968, Sea Archer fire control; **Sonar** As *Brave*; **Aircraft** 2 × Lynx HAS 3/Sea King HAS 5/EH 101; **Builders** Yarrow; **Laid down** 14 December 1983; **Launched** 14 October 1985; **Completed** 1987; **Commissioned** 1987.

Name *Cumberland* (ex-*Cumbria*); **Pennant number** F100; **Flight deck code** CD; **Builders** Yarrow; **Laid down** 20 December 1983; **Launched** 1986; **Completed** 1988; **Commissioned** 1989.

Name *Chatham*; **Pennant number** F101; **Flight deck code** CT; **Builders** Swan Hunter (Wallsend); **Laid down** 12 May 1986; **Launched** 1988; **Completed** 1990; **Commissioned** 1990.

Name Campbletown; **Pennant number** F102; **Flight deck code** CN; **Builders** Cammell Laird; **Laid down** 1985; **Launched** 1987; **Completed** 1989; **Commissioned** 1989.

An artist's impression of the Batch 3 Type 22 frigate which mounts the Mk8 114 mm gun for NGS (British Shipbuilders).

Type 22 Batch 3 (Cornwall)
Scale 1:900

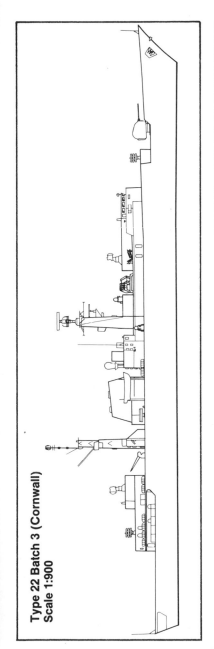

Type 23 (Duke)
Scale 1:900

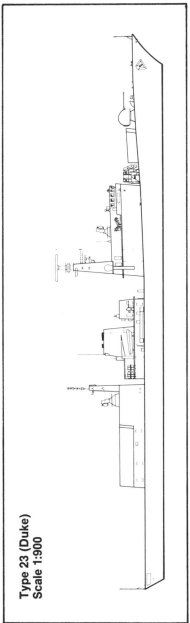

Following the experience of the Falklands' conflict, the Royal Navy has substantially improved upon the already more than adequate Batch 2 design. The main changes include the provision of the Vickers Mk 8 gun for naval gunfire support (NGS) and the McDonnell Douglas Harpoon anti-ship cruise missile has replaced the Aerospatiale MM38 Exocet. To aid gunfire direction, the British Aerospace Sea Archer fire control system has been fitted. As a close-in weapons system (CIWS), the Anglo-Dutch 30 mm Goalkeeper system has been acquired.

The Batch 3 frigates will have anti-submarine warfare as their primary role; this includes as a platform for naval helicopters up to and including the EH 101 which is scheduled to enter service in the late 1990s.

Type 23 'Duke' Class

Name *Norfolk*; **Pennant number** F230; **Flight deck code** NF; **Standard displacement** 3,000 tons; **Full displacement** 3,700 tons; **Length** 133 m; **Beam** 15 m; **Draught** 4.3 m; **Propulsion** CODLAG, 2 × Rolls-Royce Spey SM1A (34,000 shp), 4 × Paxman Valenta diesels (7,000 shp)/2 × General Electric electric motors, 2 × shafts; **Range** 7,500 nm at 15 kt; **Speed (max)** 28 kt; **Speed (cruise)** 18 kt; **Speed (patrol)** 15 kt; **Complement** 15 officers and 162 ratings; **Armament** 1 × 114 mm Vickers Mk 8 gun; 8 × Harpoon single cell launchers, 4 × Mk32 STWS-2, 1 × 32 Seawolf VLS PDMS, 4 × Sea Gnat CM, 2 × 30 mm Goalkeeper CIWS; **Sensors** 2 × 911, 1 × 996, 1 × 1007; **Sonars** 1 × 2031 TA, 1 × 2050, 1 × UAF–1 and Thorn EMI Guardian EW, IFF, SCOT, DF; **Aircraft** 2 × Lynx HAS 3/Sea King HAS 5/EH 101; **Builders** Yarrow; **Laid down** 1985; **Launched** 1987; **Completed** 1989; **Commissioned** 1989.

Name *Devonshire*; **Pennant number** F231; **Flight deck code** DE; **Builders** Swan Hunter (Wallsend); **Laid down** 1986; **Launched** 1988; **Completed** 1990; **Commissioned** 1990.

A total class of at least eight is expected to be ordered in the near future (1986–88) at a cost of approximately £200 million each.

The Type 23 frigate is the new anti-submarine escort design for the 1990s and full account of Falklands' experience has been made in the armament, sea keeping qualities, sensors, environmental control (including NBCD) and silent running for anti-submarine operations. Armament includes the Mk 8 gun mounting for NGS and the Harpoon system for over-the-horizon anti-ship operations as part of a Surface Action Group; in addition, provision has been made for two helicopters of the smaller type or the EH 101. Sensors include the new Kelvin

At RNEE '83, British Shipbuilders displayed their artist's impression of the Type 23 frigate, which includes vertical launch Sea Wolf amongst its armament (British Shipbuilders).

Hughes Type 1007 navigation radar and the Marconi Defence Systems Type 991 Seawolf guidance radar. Sea Archer fire control has again been ordered and this will be integrated with the CACS–4 action information organisation.

The propulsion system is based around the Rolls-Royce Spey engine which has been fitted to the Type 22 frigates, which the Type 23 will supplement and may eventually replace. In addition, using the experience gained in power generation aboard the '*Invincible*' Class aircraft carriers, four Paxman Valenta diesel engines have been fitted to operate with two General Electric motors to drive the ship as quietly as possible during deep water anti-submarine operations.

Although the first of the class was ordered in October 1984, considerable time had been taken to consider the original Yarrow design which was said to have been priced at £70 million, the cost of a '*Leander*' mid-life modernization.

Accommodation includes provision for training billets, especially in view of the fact that the power generation system is new; officers have their own cabins and a good standard of messing is available for ratings, away from the noise of amidships compartments.

MINES COUNTER-MEASURES VESSELS

'Hunt' Class

Name *Brecon*; **Pennant number** M29; **Standard displacement** 615 tons; **Full displacement** 725 tons; **Length (overall)** 60 m; **Beam** 9.9 m; **Draught** 2.2 m; **Propulsion** 2 × Rushton-Paxman Deltic diesels (3,800 shp), 2 × shafts; **Range** 1,500 nm at 12 kt; **Speed (max)** 16 kt; **Speed (economic)** 12 kt; **Speed (special manoeuvring)** 8 kt; **Complement** 6 officers and 39 ratings; **Armament** 1 × 40 mm Bofors GP, 2 × 7.62 mm GPMG; **Sensors** 1 × 1006; **Sonar** 1 × 2093; **Builders** Vosper Thornycroft; **Laid down** 15 September 1975; **Launched** 21 June 1978; **Completed** 1979; **Commissioned** 21 March 1980.

Name *Ledbury*; **Pennant number** M30; **Laid down** 5 October 1977; **Launched** 5 December 1979; **Completed** 1980; **Commissioned** 11 June 1981.

Name *Cattistock*; **Pennant number** M31; **Laid down** 20 June 1979; **Launched** 22 January 1981; **Completed** 5 March 1982; **Commissioned** 16 July 1982.

Name *Brocklesby*; **Pennant number** M33; **Laid down** 1980; **Launched** 12 January 1982; **Completed** 25 October 1982; **Commissioned** 3 February 1982.

Name *Dulverton*; **Pennant number** M35; **Laid down** 1981; **Launched** 3 November 1982; **Completed** 5 October 1983; **Commissioned** 3 November 1983.

Name *Bicester*; **Pennant number** M36; **Laid down** 1984; **Launched** 4 June 1985; **Completed** 1985; **Commissioned** 14 February 1986.

Name *Chiddingfold*; **Pennant number** M37; **Laid down** May 1982; **Launched** 6 October 1983; **Completed** 18 July 1984; **Commissioned** 10 August 1984.

Name *Athestone*; **Pennant number** M38; **Laid down** 1985; **Launched** 1 March 1986; **Completed** December 1986; **Commissioned** January 1987.

Name *Hurworth*; **Pennant number** M39; **Laid down** February 1983; **Launched** 25 September 1984; **Completed** June 1985; **Commissioned** June 1985.

Brecon, *the first of a new class of glass reinforced plastic mines counter-measures vessels for the Royal Navy* (Vosper Thornycroft).

Name *Cottesmore*; **Pennant number** M32; **Builders** Yarrow; **Laid down** 1981; **Launched** 9 February 1982; **Completed** 1982; **Commissioned** 24 June 1983.

Name *Middleton*; **Pennant number** M34; **Laid down** 1981; **Launched** 10 May 1982; **Completed** June 1984; **Commissioned** 15 August 1984.

Others Two more were ordered from Vosper Thornycroft in late 1985: *Berkeley* (M40) and *Quorn* (M41).

The 'Hunt' Class is the latest generation of mines counter-measures vessels (MCMV) to enter service with the Royal Navy; they are constructed of glass reinforced plastic (GRP) of revolutionary design, the largest ships in the world to be so built. Original work was carried out by Vosper Thornycroft, although two ships (*Cottesmore* and *Middleton*) have been completed at Yarrow's yard following an agreement in September 1979.

The use of GRP in the 'Hunt' Class is prompted because of the material's non-magnetic qualities and because it does not conduct electric current which may cause magnetic fields to be generated which in turn could detonate magnetic influence mines. An experimental programme for GRP hulls was commenced in 1970 with *Wilton*, to be built to the existing 'Ton' MH design. Clear resin is used

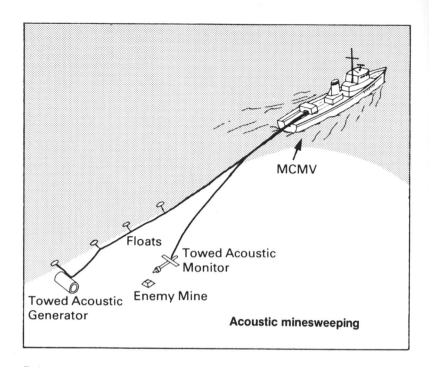

MCMV

Floats

Towed Acoustic
Monitor

Enemy Mine

Towed Acoustic
Generator

Acoustic minesweeping

Below *Exercising together in the Solent, the first two 'Hunt' Class MCMVs,* Brecon *(M29) and* Ledbury *(M30)* (RN/HMS *Daedalus*).

Above Ledbury *showing her sweep deck and minehunting gear* (RN).

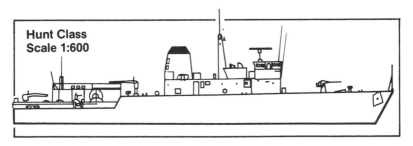

Hunt Class
Scale 1:600

Chiddingfold *on builder's trials prior to being accepted by the Royal Navy.* (Vosper Thornycroft).

in the manufacturing technique so that any faults may be immediately detected. A great deal of research effort has been put into the development of both the resin and the moulding process. The Royal Navy is the first maritime power to use GRP MCM vessels.

In terms of magnetic signatures, the ships are well within current NATO guidelines and the class has been extensively involved in trials and exercises with NATO neighbours, particularly the NATO Standing Force Channel in the mines counter-measures role. After initial trials in *Brecon*, it is understood that the ballast arrangements were amended to provide better seakeeping qualities.

The ships' role is to replace the older and ageing 'Ton' Class MCMV in both the minehunting (MH) and minesweeping (CMS) tasks, combining the equipment needed in one hull. For MH tasks, the ships have been equipped with the French PAP104 submersible, equipped with a camera and to drop mine detonation charges.

The class is designed for three types of mine disposal: sweeping for moored mines so that they come to the surface where they can be destroyed by gunfire; sweeping with acoustic and magnet influence sets to detonate bottom or special mines; hunting the mines with Type 2093 sonar and using the submersible or clearance divers to dismantle or destroy mines.

'Ton' Class Minehunters

Name *Bronington*; **Pennant number** M1115; **Standard displacement** 360 tons; **Full displacement** 425 tons; **Length (overall)** 46.3 m; **Beam** 8.8 m; **Draught** 2.5 m; **Propulsion** 2 × Mirrlees diesels (2,500 bhp) or 2 × Napier Deltic diesels (3,000 bhp), 2 × shafts; **Range** 2,300 nm at 12 kt; **Speed** 15 kt; **Complement** 5 officers and 33 ratings; **Armament** 1 × 40 mm Bofors GP Mk9, up to 2 × 20 mm Oerlikon GP, 3 × 7.62 mm GPMG; **Sensors** 1 × 1006, Echo Sounder; **Sonar** 1 × 193; **Builders** Cook Welton & Gemmell; **Commissioned** 4 June 1954.

Name *Hubberston*; **Pennant number** M1147; **Builders** Fleetland Shipyards; **Commissioned** 14 October 1955.

Name *Brereton*; **Pennant number** M1113; **Builders** Richards Ironworks; **Commissioned** 9 July 1954; Currently Mersey (10 MCM Squadron Royal Naval Reserve).

Name *Bossington*; **Pennant number** M1133; **Builders** Thornycroft; **Commissioned** 11 December 1956.

Name *Iveston*; **Pennant number** M1151; **Sonar** 1 × 193M; **Builders** Philip (Dartmouth); **Commissioned** 29 June 1955.

Name *Brinton*; **Pennant number** M1114; **Builders** Cook Welton & Gemmell; **Commissioned** 4 March 1954.

Once the command of HRH the Prince of Wales, Bronington *is a 'Ton' Class minehunter serving with the Second MCM Squadron at Portsmouth* (RN/ FPU).

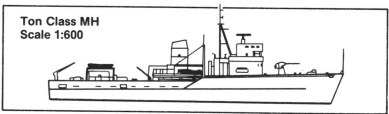

Ton Class MH
Scale 1:600

Top *Dressed overall for the Queen's birthday,* Nurton *passes the Isle of Wight prior to entering Portsmouth Harbour* (RN).

Name *Gavinton*; **Pennant number** M1140; **Builders** J.S. Doig (Grimsby); **Commissioned** 14 July 1954; Paid off 1986.

Name *Kedleston*; **Pennant number** M1153; **Builders** Pickersgill; **Commissioned** 2 July 1955; Currently Forth (10 MCM Squadron Royal Naval Reserve).

Name *Kellington*; **Pennant number** M1154; **Builders** Pickersgill; **Commissioned** 4 November 1955; Currently Sussex (10 MCM Squadron Royal Naval Reserve).

Name *Nurton*; **Pennant number** M1166; **Builders** Harland & Wolff; **Commissioned** 21 August 1957.

Name *Kirkliston*; **Pennant number** M1157; **Builders** Harland & Wolff; **Commissioned** 21 August 1954.

Name *Sheraton*; **Pennant number** M1181; **Builders** White's (Southampton); **Commissioned** 24 August 1956.

Name *Maxton*; **Pennant number** M1165; **Builders** Harland & Wolff; **Commissioned** 19 February 1957.

'Ton' Class Coastal Minesweepers

Name *Cuxton*; **Pennant number** M1125; **Complement** 4 officers and 25 ratings; **Builders** Camper Nicholson; **Commissioned** 1953.

Name *Upton*; **Pennant number** M1187; **Builders** Thornycroft; **Commissioned** 24 July 1956; Currently serves with the Fisheries Protection Squadron.

Bottom *Wearing the emblem of the Tenth MCM Squadron, manned by the Royal Naval Reserve,* Upton *is classed as a coastal minesweeper* (RN).

Ton Class CMS
Scale 1:600

Passing Gibraltar during an RNR deployment to the Straits, Wotton *shows some of the minesweeping gear aboard* (RN/FOSNI).

Name *Soberton*; **Pennant number** M1200; **Builders** Fleetlands (Gosport); **Commissioned** 17 September 1957; Currently serving with the Fisheries Protection Squadron.

Name *Crichton*; **Pennant number** M1124; **Builders** J.S. Doig (Grimsby); **Commissioned** 23 April 1954; Currently serving with the Fisheries Protection Squadron.

Name *Shavington*; **Pennant number** M1180; **Builders** White's (Southampton); **Commissioned** 1 March 1956; Currently Ulster (10 MCM Squadron Royal Naval Reserve).

Name *Wotton*; **Pennant number** M1195; **Builders** Philip (Dartmouth); **Commissioned** 13 June 1957; Currently London (10 MCM Squadron Royal Naval Reserve).

Name *Glasserton*; **Pennant number** M1141; **Builders** J.S. Doig (Grimsby); **Commissioned** 31 December 1954; Currently serving as immobile tender for London Division Royal Naval Reserve.

'Ton' Class MCMV

Name *Wilton*; **Pennant number** M1116; **Standard displacement** As *Bronington*; **Full displacement** 450 tons; **Length (overall)** 46.3 m; **Beam** 8.9

m; **Propulsion** 2 × Napier Deltic diesels (3,000 bhp), 2 × shafts; **Range** 2,300 nm at 13 kt; **Speed** 16 kt; **Armament** 1 × 40 mm Bofors Mk 7; **Sensors** 1 × 975, 1 × 955M IFF; **Sonar** 1 × 193; **Builders** Vosper Thornycroft; **Laid down** 7 August 1970; **Launched** 18 January 1972; **Completed** 1973; **Commissioned** 14 July 1973.

Designed and built as a result of the mine warfare situation which developed after the Second World War, particularly in the Korean conflict 1950–53, with John Thornycroft's yard (now part of Vosper Thornycroft) as the design lead. The hull is double-skinned mahogany with aluminium structures for low magnetic signature; the original copper sheathing has been replaced by nylon during refit.

The 'Ton' Class has provided the backbone of British post-war mines warfare until the development of the 'Hunt' Class, but duties have included patrol (in the Persian Gulf, Hong Kong and offshore), fisheries protection and providing seagoing vessels for the Royal Naval Reserve. Many have now been in commission for more than

Bottom Wilton, *the world's first plastic MCMV, at Portsmouth* (Paul Beaver).

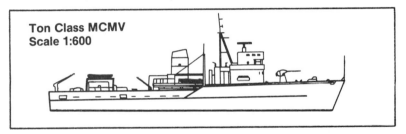

Ton Class MCMV
Scale 1:600

thirty years and the class will probably be withdrawn operationally by 1991; at least 37 have been handed over to friendly navies and others have been paid off for scrapping.

In the early 1960s, the class was sub-divided into minehunters and coastal minesweepers, with several being converted for patrol duties without the benefit of sweep gear. The minehunting role is being taken over by the 'Hunt' and 'Sandown' Classes and the minesweeping role by the 'River' Class.

Wilton is a specially built trials ship for the 'Hunt' Class GRP construction technique, using equipment from *Derriton* (scrapped); used in the Suez Canal clearance operations in 1973.

Minehunters These vessels use special sonar to detect objects on the seabed and to 'map' frequently used channels to detect the presence of recently introduced mines and other explosives. To identify the mine, the sonar can be used or a television-equipped PAP104 submersible, or specialist clearance divers.

Minesweepers This role has to a large degree been overshadowed by the MH; sweep gear is carried on the quarterdeck and trailed behind the craft to release tethered mines or detonate influence types.

'River' Class Minesweepers

Name *Waveney*; **Pennant number** M2003; **Full displacement** 890 tons; **Length** 47.5 m; **Beam** 10.5 m; **Draught** 2.9 m; **Propulsion** 2 × Rushton RKCM diesels (3,000 bhp), 2 × shafts; **Range** 2,500 nm at 12 kt; **Speed** 14 kt; **Complement** 7 officers and 23 ratings; **Armament** 1 × 40 mm Bofors Mk 3; **Sensors** 2 × Racal 1226; **Builders** Richards; **Launched** 8 September 1983; **Completed** 2 May 1984; **Commissioned** 12 July 1984; Allocated South Wales RNR.

Name *Carron*; **Pennant number** M2004; **Launched** 23 September 1983; **Completed** 20 June 1984; **Commissioned** 29 September 1984; Allocated Severn RNR.

Name *Dovey*; **Pennant number** M2005; **Launched** 7 December 1983; **Completed** 30 October 1984; **Commissioned** December 1984; Allocated Clyde RNR.

Name *Helford*; **Pennant number** M2006; **Laid down** 12 October 1983; **Launched** 16 May 1984; **Completed** March 1985; **Commissioned** May 1985; Allocated Ulster RNR.

Name *Humber;* **Pennant number** M2007; **Launched** 17 May 1984; **Completed** April 1985; **Commissioned** May 1985; Allocated London RNR.

Above Waveney *is the first of a new class of mine countermeasure vessels for the Royal Naval Reserve, replacements for the 'Ton' Class* (RN/HMS Osprey).

Below Carron *is attached to Severn RNR at Bristol but was photographed leaving Portsmouth* (Mike Lennon).

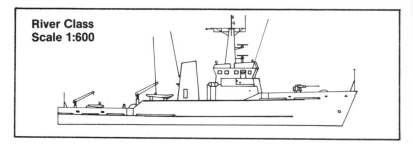

**River Class
Scale 1:600**

Name *Blackwater*; **Pennant number** M2008; **Laid down** 16 January 1984; **Launched** 29 August 1984; **Completed** March 1985; **Commissioned** 14 June 1985; Allocated Fishery Protection Squadron.

Name *Itchen*; **Pennant number** M2009; **Launched** 30 October 1984; **Commissioned** September 1985; Allocated Solent RNR.

Name *Helmsdale*; **Pennant number** M2010; **Launched** 11 January 1985; **Completed** 1986; Allocated Tay RNR.

Name *Orwell*; **Pennant number** M2011; **Launched** 5 February 1985; **Completed** 1986; Allocated Tyne RNR.

Name *Ribble*; **Pennant number** M2012; **Launched** 7 May 1985; **Completed** 1986; Allocated Mersey RNR.

Name *Spey*; **Pennant number** M2013; **Laid down** November 1984; **Launched** 22 May 1985; **Completed** 1986; Allocated Forth RNR.

Name *Arun*; **Pennant number** M2014; **Laid down** February 1985; **Launched** 20 August 1985; **Completed** 1986; Allocated Sussex RNR.

Cost-effective minesweepers designed for operation by the Royal Naval Reserve, the 'River' Class have all been built at Lowestoft or Great Yarmouth by Richards Limited. The design includes steep hulls for deep team sweeping using the WS Mk 9 sweep gear, using techniques which were developed by the converted trawlers *St David* (M07) and *Venturer* (M08) during 1978–84.

'Sandown' Class Minehunter

Name *Sandown*; **Pennant number** M231; **Standard displacement** 450 tons; **Full displacement** 492 tons; **Length** 50 m; **Beam** 9 m; **Draught** 2 m; **Propulsion** 2 × Paxman diesels (3,000 bhp), 2 × electric motors with thrusters, 2 × shafts; **Range** Not known; **Speed** 16 kt; **Complement** 7 officers

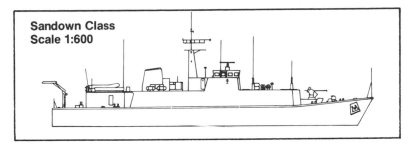

Sandown Class
Scale 1:600

and 33 ratings; **Armament** 1 × 20 mm Oerlikon GAM-B01; **Sensors** 1 × Navigation radar; **Sonar** 1 × dipping; **Builders** Vosper Thornycroft; **Laid down** 1986; **Launched** 1986; **Completed** 1987; **Commissioned** 1988.

It was announced at the Royal Naval Equipment Exhibition in September 1983 that Vosper Thornycrooft would design and develop a new class of single role minehunter, built with a glass reinforced plastic hull. In January 1984, the design received Admiralty approval and a tender was invited from Vosper Thornycroft. Equipment specified includes good quality navigation radar, dipping sonar transducer, remotely controlled submersible for laying explosives and carrying a television camera, side-scan sonar for classification and facilities to support clearance divers. A class of twelve is thought to be planned.

An artist's impression of the 'Sandown' *Class single role minehunter to be built for the Royal Navy by Vosper Thornycroft.*

MINES COUNTERMEASURES SUPPORT SHIP

'Abdiel' Class

Name *Abdiel*; **Pennant number** N21; **Standard displacement** 1,375 tons; **Full displacement** 1,500 tons; **Length (overall)** 80.8 m; **Beam** 11.7 m; **Draught** 3 m; **Propulsion** 2 × Paxman diesels (2,690 bhp), 2 × shafts; **Range** 4,500 nm at 12 kt; **Speed** 16 kt; **Complement** 8 officers and 90 ratings; **Armament** 1 × 40 mm Bofors Mk 9 (when carried), 44 × mines; **Sensors** 1 × 1006, DF; **Sonar** 1 × 193M; **Aircraft** Flight deck space; **Builders** Thornycroft; **Laid down** 23 May 1966; **Launched** 27 January 1967; **Completed** 1967; **Commissioned** 17 October 1967; **Modernization** 1978.

This is a multi-role ship, designed to act as a floating base for minehunting and minesweeping support operations; this was put into effect during the Suez Canal clearance operations in 1974 and again off the Falkland Islands in 1982–83. The ship is also designed for laying both operational and practice mines, including the Marconi Sea Urchin.

During March 1984, *Oil Endeavour* was chartered by the Ministry of Defence for operations in the Middle East and the offshore support vessel, *Kent Salvage*, was taken up from trade in February of that year. The charters continued until 1985.

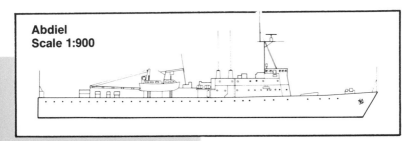

Abdiel
Scale 1:900

Abdiel, *in company with a 'Ton' Class MCMV, encounters rough weather* (RN).

OFFSHORE PATROL VESSELS

Ice Patrol Ship

Name *Endurance*; **Pennant number** A171; **Flight deck code** E; **Measured displacement** 2,641 tons; **Full displacement** 3,600 tons; **Length (overall)** 93 m; **Beam** 14 m; **Draught** 5.5 m; **Propulsion** 1 × Burmeister & Wain diesel (3,220 hp), 1 × shaft; **Range** 12,000 nm at 14.5 kt; **Speed** 14.5 kt; **Complement** 13 officers and 106 ratings, 12 passengers; **Armament** 2 × 20 mm Oerlikon GP; **Sensors** Marisat, 1 × 1006; **Aircraft** 2 × Lynx HAS 3; **Builders** Krogerwerft (Rendsburg); **Laid down** 1955; **Launched** May 1956; **Completed** December 1956 (as *Anita Dan*); **Purchased** 20 February 1967; **Converted** 1968; **Major refits** 1978, 1983, 1986–87.

Purchased by the Admiralty to act as the Falkland Islands guardship and as the British ice patrol ship, providing a presence in the Antarctic during the southern hemisphere summer, *Endurance* was at the centre of the 1982 South Atlantic crisis. The ship was the only British warship in the area when the Argentines invaded both South Georgia and the Falkland Islands.

She is painted red and white for ease of identification and her helicopters, currently Wasp but to be replaced by Lynx in 1987–88, are also painted with dayglo panels in case of forced landing on the ice. Although nominally the only Royal Naval ship equipped to work in the ice, she was destined for disposal in 1982 (a contributory factor to the Argentine invasion decision) but will now continue in service indefinitely.

'Castle' Class

Name *Leeds Castle*; **Pennant number** P258; **Flight deck code** LC; **Standard displacement** 1,450 tons; **Length (overall)** 81 m; **Beam** 11 m; **Draught** 3 m; **Propulsion** 2 × Rushton diesels (2,820 bhp) with controllable pitch propellor; **Range** 10,000 nm at 10 kt; **Speed (max)** 20 kt; **Speed (cruising)** 15 kt; **Complement** 6 officers and 34 ratings; **Armament** 1 × 40 mm Bofors, 4 × 7.62 mm GPMG; **Sensors** 1 × 1006, DF, Omega, CANE, Satcomm; **Aircraft** Flight deck for Sea King; **Builders** Hall Russell; **Laid down** November 1979; **Launched** 29 October 1980; **Completed** 25 August 1981; **Commissioned** 15 October 1981.

Name *Dumbarton Castle*; **Pennant number** P265; **Laid down** 1980; **Launched** 3 June 1981; **Completed** February 1982; **Commissioned** 26 March 1982.

Part of Endurance's *Embarked Detachment in Falklands waters prior to the Argentine invasion* (RN).

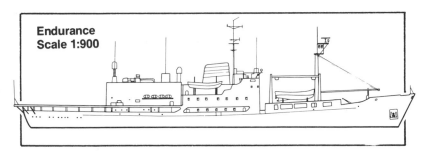

Endurance
Scale 1:900

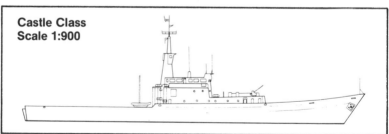

**Castle Class
Scale 1:900**

Top *Seen off Rosyth,* Leeds Castle *was the first of two Offshore Patrol Vessels designed for this specialist task.*

Built originally as a private venture, the 'Castle' Class consists of two Offshore Patrol Vessels (OPVs) which cost some £12 million each and are operated by the Fisheries Protection Squadron, based at Rosyth. They are long-ranged and more seaworthy than the 'Ton' Class which they are replacing for certain special roles.

The design includes provision for helicopters up to about 25,000 lb (11,340 kg), but only in terms of a flight deck and refuelling equipment; there is no hangar facility in the design. The ship has been equipped with stabilizers for the helicopter role and full recovery facilities (glide slope indicator and horizon bar) have been fitted for night operations. The original plan to fit the 76 mm Oto Melara guns seems to have been dropped but the ships have facilities for a minelaying role.

'Peacock' Class

Name *Peacock*; **Pennant number** P239; **Standard displacement** 652 tons; **Full displacement** 700 tons; **Length (overall)** 62.6 m; **Beam** 10 m; **Draught** 2.7 m; **Propulsion** 2 × APE Crossley Pielstick 18 diesels (14,000 shp), 2 × shafts; **Range** 2,500 nm at 17 kt; **Speed (max)** 28 kt; **Speed (cruise)** 17 kt; **Complement** 6 officers and 38 ratings; **Armament** 1 × 76 mm Oto Melara, 4 × 7.62 mm GPMG; **Sensors** 1× 1006, Sea Archer; **Builders** Hall Russell; **Laid down** January 1982; **Launched** 1 December 1982; **Completed** June 1983; **Commissioned** 14 July 1984.

Preparing to board a suspect vessel, Peacock's *Searider rigid inflatable is swung out* (JSPRS Hong Kong).

101

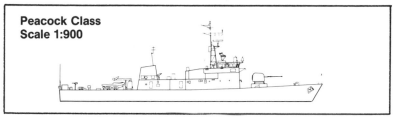

Peacock Class
Scale 1:900

Left *The Hong Kong Squadron at sea together off the Colony; note the 76 mm Oto Melara gun* (JSPRS Hong Kong).

Name *Plover*; **Pennant number** P240; **Laid down** 1982; **Launched** 12 April 1983; **Completed** 1983; **Commissioned** 20 July 1984.

Name *Starling*; **Pennant number** P241; **Laid down** 1982; **Launched** 7 September 1983; **Completed** 1984; **Commissioned** 7 August 1984.

Name *Swallow*; **Pennant number** P242; **Laid down** 1983; **Launched** 30 March 1984; **Completed** 17 October 1984; **Commissioned** 16 November 1984.

Name *Swift*; **Pennant number** P243; **Laid down** 1983; **Launched** 11 September 1984; **Completed** 1985; **Commissioned** 1985.

Designed and built by Hall Russell at Aberdeen, the 'Peacock' Class Hong Kong patrol craft were 75 per cent funded by the Hong Kong Government and the five ships are now operational in defence of the Colony and in support of the Governor. All were ordered in June 1981 to replace the converted 'Ton' Class patrol vessels which had been in the Colony since 1971.

The class has been well armed with the 76 mm gun, controlled by the British Aerospace Sea Archer and linked to the Type 1006 radar. Additional equipment includes the Kelvin Hughes MS45 Mk II Echo Sounder, the Racal-Decca Navigation and Racal Tacticom marine and ship-to-shore radios. From late 1986, the craft were also equipped with the GEC Avionics V3800 thermal imaging sensor for long-range target detection, identification and tracking by day or night; the sensor is mounted on the optical fire director and is controlled from below decks and displayed on a video. Part of the patrol task of the 'Peacock' Class is in support of the Royal Hong Kong Police so rapid and effective communications are important.

The main role of the class is the patrol and enforcement of law in the Colony's waters, supporting the RHKP Marine unit in anti-smuggling operations, and self-deployment to neighbouring countries in the South China Sea. In the police support role, the vessels act as radar pickets and as pick-up craft for illegal immigrants (IIs). The ships also act as training billets for Midshipmen but it has never been expected that even these patrol craft would be able to protect the Colony from a determined seaborne invasion.

The class has the ability for Replenishment at Sea (RAS).

'Island' Class

Name *Jersey*; **Pennant number** P295; **Standard displacement** 925 tons; **Full displacement** 1,250 tons; **Length (overall)** 59.6 m; **Beam** 10.9 m; **Draught** 4.3 m; **Propulsion** 2 × Rushton RKCM diesels (4,380 shp), 1 × shaft; **Range** 7,000 nm at 12 kt; **Speed** 17 kt; **Complement** 5 officers and 30 ratings; **Armament** 1 × 40 mm Bofors GP Mk 3, 2 × 7.62 mm GPMG; **Sensors** 1 × 1006; **Builders** Hall Russell; **Ordered** 2 July 1975; **Launched** 18 March 1976; **Completed** 1976; **Commissioned** 15 October 1976.

Name *Orkney*; **Pennant number** P299; **Launched** 29 June 1976; **Completed** 1977; **Commissioned** 25 February 1977.

Alderney *at sea immediately after RN acceptance* (Hall Russell).

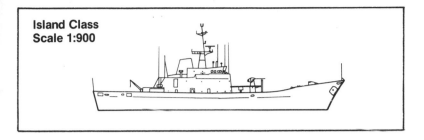

Island Class
Scale 1:900

Name *Shetland*; **Pennant number P298; Launched** 22 October 1976; **Completed** 1977; **Commissioned** 14 July 1977.

Name *Guernsey*; **Pennant number** P297; **Laid down** 14 May 1976; **Launched** 17 February 1977; **Completed** 22 September 1977; **Commissioned** 28 October 1977.

Name *Lindisfarne*; **Pennant number** P300; **Launched** 1 June 1977; **Completed** 1978; **Commissioned** 3 March 1978.

Name *Anglesey*; **Pennant number** P277; **Laid down** 6 February 1978; **Launched** 18 October 1978; **Completed** 1979; **Commissioned** 1 June 1979.

Name *Alderney*; **Pennant number** P278; **Laid down** 11 June 1978; **Launched** 27 February 1979; **Completed** 1979; **Commissioned** 6 October 1979.

The 'Island' Class offshore patrol vessels are designed to operate in the protection of British interests in the protection of the 270,000 square miles (669,300 sq km) economic zone, particularly dealing with fisheries protection and the defence of offshore oil/gas platforms. The design was based on the successful Scottish department of Agriculture and Fisheries *'Jura'* Class also built by Hall Russell at Aberdeen; *Jura* was operated by the Royal Navy from Rosyth in the mid-1970s with the former tug, *Reward*, until the first 'Islands' became available.

The first five of the class were ordered in July 1975 and despite criticism that the ships were not fast enough to catch rogue trawlers nor to respond to offshore terrorist incidents, a further two were ordered on 21 October 1977. All now have improved bilge-keels and stabilizers.

The ships are powered by Rushton diesels which give good fuel economy and they are fitted with CANE 1 (Computer Assisted Navigation Equipment) which allows the exact position of the ship and any alleged illegally fishing trawler to be recorded for possible use in

Court later. On average, one of these craft (all of which are attached to the Offshore Division of the Fisheries Protection Squadron at Rosyth) will inspect 150 trawlers and other craft in any twelve-month period.

'Protector' Class

Name *Protector*; **Pennant number** P244; **Gross displacement** 802 tons; **Deadweight displacement** 1,030 tons; **Length** 58.4 m; **Beam** 12 m; **Draught** 4.5 m; **Propulsion** 2 × Polar diesels (6,160 shp), 2 × shafts; **Range** 7,000 nm at 12 kt; **Speed** 18 kt; **Complement** 4 officers and 20 ratings; **Armament** 2 × 40 mm Bofors GP, 2 × 7.62 mm GPMG; **Sensors** 1 × 1006; **Builders** Drypool (Selby); **Completed** 1975; **Purchased** 1983; **Commissioned** 21 October 1983.

Name *Guardian*; **Pennant number** P245; **Builders** Beverley Shipyard (Yorkshire); **Completed** January 1975; **Purchased** 1983; **Commissioned** 21 October 1983.

Bottom *Photographed in the Falkland Islands, the patrol vessel* Protector *shows some evidence of use* (Mike Lennon).

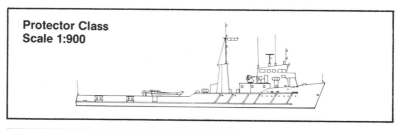

Protector Class
Scale 1:900

Guardian *leaves Portsmouth for duties in the South Atlantic. Note the Searider and 40mm Bofors guns* (Mike Lennon).

'Sentinel' Class

Name *Sentinel*; **Pennant number** P246; **Standard displacement** 1,710 tons; **Full displacement** 2,100 tons; **Length** 60.5 m; **Beam** 13.3 m; **Draught** 4.5 m; **Propulsion** 2 × Atlas MaK diesels (7,700 shp), 2 × shafts; **Range** 7,000 nm at 12 kt; **Speed** 14 kt; **Complement** 5 officers and 21 ratings; **Armament** 2 × 40 mm Bofors GP, 3 × 7.62 mm GPMG, 2 × 2-in SRBOC launchers; **Sensors** 1 × 1006; **Builders** Husumwerft; **Completed** 1975; **Purchased** 1983; **Commissioned** 14 January 1984.

The Falkland Islands patrol Vessels were announced in the 1983 Defence White Paper and were purchased to defend the inshore waters around the Falkland Islands thus relieving other Royal Navy vessels of this more specialist task. The ships were originally operated by Seaforth Maritime for various owners on oil rig support duties, and converted at Cardiff and by Tyne Shiprepair. They took over the inshore role from a number of temporarily impressed captured Argentine craft.

Above Sentinel *on duty patrolling the Falkland Islands coastal waters* (Mike Lennon).

Right Cygnet *patrolling offshore Northern Ireland* (RN/HMS *Osprey*).

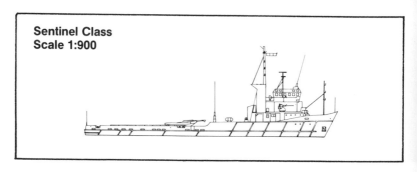

Sentinel Class
Scale 1:900

Equipped with small arms and Avon SR3M Searider/Pacific 22 rigid inflatable craft for boarding and inspection duties, the craft are expected to remain in service at least ten years as part of the 'Fortress Falklands' policy. *Sentinel* has an ice strengthened bow and is the leader of the Falkland Islands Patrol Squadron.

Apart from surveillance, the Squadron is engaged in ferrying stores and troops around the islands and forms an important 'hearts and minds' link with outlying settlements. Ships' companies serve between four and six months, and the complement can include a Royal Marines detachment. The ships use RFA *Diligence* for assisted maintenance and as a depot ship.

Former names: *Protector* (*Seaforth Saga*); *Guardian* (*Seaforth Champion*); *Sentinel* (*Seaforth Warrior*).

'Bird' Class

Name *Kingfisher*; **Pennant number** P260; **Full displacement** 194 tons; **Length (overall)** 36.6 m; **Beam** 7 m; **Draught** 2 m; **Propulsion** 2 × Paxman diesels (4,200 shp), 2 × shafts; **Range** 2,000 nm at 14 kt; **Speed** 21 kt; **Complement** 4 officers and 19 ratings; **Armament** 1 × 40 mm Bofors GP Mk 9, 2 × 7.62 mm GPMG; **Sensors** 1 × 1006; **Builders** Richard Dunston; **Laid down** 1974; **Launched** 20 September 1974; **Completed** 1975; **Commissioned** 8 October 1975.

Name *Cygnet*; **Pennant number** P261; **Laid down** 1975; **Launched** 6 October 1975; **Completed** July 1976; **Commissioned** 8 July 1976.

Originally designed with the 'Seal' Class Royal Air Force Maritime service (disbanded in 1985) rescue craft in mind, the 'Bird' Class have enhanced seakeeping qualities, including the use of stabilizers. Four of the class were built and two are now training vessels with the Britannia Royal Naval College, Dartmouth. The class was found unsuitable for Fisheries Protection work and all four were transferred to new duties as Northern Ireland Patrol Craft from the Inshore Division.

Other Northern Ireland Patrol Craft are *Peterel* (P262) and *Sandpiper* (P263); *Redpole* (ex-*Sea Otter*), ex-RAF 'Seal' Class, was transferred in March 1985; she is slightly lighter at 159 tons displacement. She was commissioned into the RAF in August 1967.

SURVEY CRAFT

'Hecla' Class

Name *Hecla*; **Pennant number** A133; **Flight deck code** HL; **Standard displacement** 1,915 tons; **Full displacement** 2,733 tons; **Length (overall)** 79.3 m; **Beam** 15 m; **Draught** 4.7 m; **Propulsion** 3 × Paxman Ventura diesels (3,840 bhp), 1 × electric motor (2,000 shp), 1 × shaft; **Range** 12,000 nm at 11 kt; **Speed** 14 kt; **Complement** 12 officers and 105 ratings; **Armament** None; **Sensors** 1 × 1006; **Aircraft** 1 × Wasp HAS 1; **Builders** Yarrow; **Laid down** 6 May 1964; **Launched** 2 December 1964; **Completed** 1965; **Commissioned** 9 September 1965.

Name *Hecate*; **Pennant number** A137; **Flight deck code** HT; **Armament** 2 × 20 mm Oerlikon GP (for South Atlantic); **Laid down** 26 October 1964; **Launched** 31 March 1965; **Completed** October 1965; **Commissioned** 20 December 1965.

Hydra (A144) was paid off in April 1986 and sold to Indonesia.

Hecate *at sea* (RN/PFU).

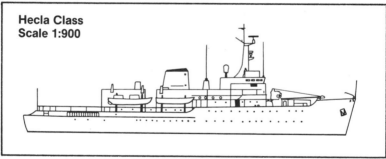

Top Hydra *in full survey ship colours* (RN/FPU).

'Improved Hecla' Class

Name *Herald*; **Pennant number** A138; **Flight deck code** HE; **Standard displacement** 2,000 tons; **Full displacement** 2,945 tons; **Length and Beam** As *Hecla*; **Draught** 5 m; **Complement** 12 officers and 106 ratings; **Armament** 2 × 20 mm Oerlikon GP (for South Atlantic); **Builders** Robb Caledon; **Laid down** 9 November 1972; **Launched** 4 October 1973; **Completed** 31 October 1974; **Commissioned** 22 November 1974.

A successful design of merchant-hulled ocean survey craft, with

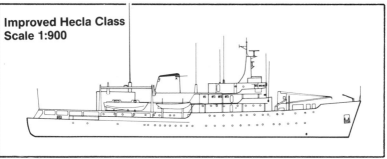

Improved Hecla Class
Scale 1:900

Top Herald *in her guise as a Patrol Vessel for the South Georgia and Falklands dependency, during the continuing support of Garrison Falklands* (Robin Walker).

good stability and fuel economy, for survey, oceanographic and hydrographic work in connection with naval operations worldwide, including the detailed charting of the sea bed for SSBN operations. The ability to operate a Westland Wasp helicopter has greatly increased the flexibility of these craft to support survey bases; in addition two 9.5 m survey craft, a launch and a Land Rover vehicle are carried.

Special equipment for the role includes Marconi Elliot Hydroplot, Hi-Fix, Satellite Navigation, Decca Pulse 8, Decca Navigator Mainchain, La-Coste Romberg Gravimeter and Baringer Magnometer. Coring and bathythermal equipment is available. Onboard are specialist workshops, a photographic studio, drawing office and special chartroom. The helicopter is hangared.

Propulsion is by diesel-electric drive which can be controlled from the bridge during delicate survey operations, or linked to the satellite and other advanced navigation sensors. The single shaft is augmented by bow thrusters for manoeuvring.

All four vessels have acted as hospital, sea ambulance and casualty evacuation ferries in the South Atlantic, with *Hecate* and *Herald* acting as patrol ships in 1982, 1983 and 1984, when *Endurance* was under maintenance and refit; both were fitted with light guns during this period. *Herald* relieved *Endurance* in April 1983. During service in the South Atlantic the ships were either painted with the Red Cross for hospital work or in overall sea grey as guard ships. The normal appearance is white hull/upperworks and a buff funnel.

'Bulldog' Class

Name *Bulldog*; **Pennant number** A317; **Standard displacement** 800 tons; **Full displacement** 1,088 tons; **Length (overall)** 60.1 m; **Beam** 11.4 m; **Draught** 3.6 m; **Propulsion** 4 × Lister Blackstone diesels (660 bhp each), 2 × shafts; **Range** 4,000 nm at 12 kt, **Speed** 15 kt; **Complement** 4 officers and 34 ratings; **Armament** None (fitted for 2 × 20 mm Oerlikon GP); **Sensors** 1 × 1007; **Builders** Brooke Marine; **Launched** 12 July 1967; **Completed** 1968; **Completed** 1968; **Commissioned** 21 March 1968.

Name *Beagle*; **Pennant number** A319; **Launched** 7 September 1967; **Completed** 1968; **Commissioned** 9 May 1968.

Name *Fox*; **Pennant number** A320; **Launched** 6 November 1967; **Completed** 1968; **Commissioned** 11 July 1968.

Name *Fawn*; **Pennant number** A325; **Launched** 29 February 1968; **Completed** 10 September 1968; **Commissioned** 4 October 1968.

Name *Roebuck*; **Pennant number** A130; Details as for *Bulldog*, except: **Full displacement** 1,500 tons; **Length** 63.9 m; **Beam** 13 m; **Draught** 3.8 m; **Propulsion** 2 × Mirrlees Blackstone diesels (3,040 bhp), 2 × shafts; **Speed** 16 kt; **Complement** 7 officers and 40 ratings; **Laid down** 1984; **Launched** 14 November 1985; **Completed** 30 August 1986; **Commissioned** 3 October 1986.

Bulldog Class
Scale 1:900

Top *Fawn in an unusual non-working pose, dressed overall.*

Coastal variants of the '*Hecla*' Class, these craft were designed for operations overseas but have borne the brunt of the surveying required for the North and Celtic Seas oil and gas exploration. No helicopter facilities are fitted

Using a merchant hull, the class is stable and designed for all-weather operations, being of all-welded construction with a bulbous underwater bow and the high flared forecastle of a good seakeeper. A passive stabilizer system of anti-rolling tanks is fitted and there are twin rudders.

The ships are powered by eight-cylinder diesel engines driving two variable pitch propellers through reduction gearing. The service cruising speed is 15 kt and the propeller pitch and engine revolutions are controlled from the bridge or machinery control room; an autopilot is fitted.

Specialist equipment includes echo sounders, Marconi Hydro-search sector scanning fisherman's sonar (to search for, locate and classify wrecks and underwater rock pinnacles – a particular hazard for large oil carriers), Hi-Fix portable electronic surveying equipment, Decca radar with precision ranging attachment and two 9.5 m survey boats with echo sounders; *Roebuck* is fitted with Marconi Hydro-search and Waverly side scan sonar.

The original four vessels were designed to work in pairs overseas, *Bulldog* with *Beagle* and *Fox* with *Fawn*. Because of the increased level of work caused by the oil exploration around the British coasts, *Roebuck* was ordered on 18 May 1984.

'Gleaner' Class

Name *Gleaner*; **Pennant number** A86; **Standard displacement** 22 tons; **Length** 14.8 m; **Beam** 4.7 m; **Draught** 1.3 m; **Propulsion** 2 × Rolls-Royce diesels (524 hp), 2 × shafts with 1 × Perkins diesel (72 hp), 1 × central shaft; **Speed (max)** 14 kt; **Speed (Perkins)** 7 kt; **Complement** 1 officer and 4 ratings; **Builders** Emsworth Shipyard; **Commissioned** 5 December 1983.

HM Survey Motor Launch (HMSML) *Gleaner* was commissioned to replace the three 'E' inshore survey craft which paid off on 31 December 1984 and *Woodlark* and *Waterwitch* which paid off in early 1985. Although of limited range and endurance, the craft is ideal for surveying and updating charts of port approaches and such areas as the Thames Estuary and Dover Straits.

The survey service has been forced to charter additional craft to support the increased work caused by the needs of the offshore oil industry and because of the need to re-survey and increase covering for the introduction of the Trident submarines. It is understood that additional inshore survey craft will be purchased and supplemented with hovercraft.

The new survey launch, Gleaner (RN/FPU).

DIVING SUPPORT AND SEABED OPERATIONS SHIPS

'Challenger' Class

Name *Challenger*; **Pennant number** K07; **Flight deck code** CH; **Standard displacement** 6,500 tons; **Full displacement** 7,185 tons; **Length** 134.1 m; **Beam** 18 m; **Draught** 5 m; **Propulsion** 5 × Rushton diesels (6,200 bhp), 2 × Voith-Schneider aft, 3 × thrusters forward; **Range** 8,000 nm at 10 kt; **Speed** 15 kt; **Complement** 185 (including diving party); **Sensors** 1 × 1006; **Sonar** 1 × 193M; **Builders** Scotts; **Laid down** 1979; **Launched** 19 May 1981; **Completed** 13 July 1984; **Commissioned** 20 August 1984.

Designed to carry out full saturation diving and seabed operations, including survey and submarine rescue, the primary role of the ship will be the recovery of objects from the seabed, using such equipment as the specially designed diving bell which is lowered and recovered through the amidships well. The stern davits have provision for a submersible craft. The ship uses a dynamic position system, assisted by the bow thrusters and the Voith-Schneider cycloidal propellers aft.

Left and above *Two views of* Challenger, *the Royal Navy's new seabed operations ship; note the large stern davits and associated equipment* (Mike Lennon).

Name *Seaforth Clansman*; **Pennant number** None; **Flight deck code** SC; **Standard displacement** 1,180 tons; **Full displacement** 1,977 tons; **Length** 78.6 m; **Beam** 14.12 m; **Draught** 5 m; **Propulsion** 4 × Mirrlees diesels (7,320 bhp), 2 × shafts, 2 × bow thrusters; **Speed** 13 kt; **Sensors** Commercial radar; **Builders** Cochranes (Selby); **Completed** 1977; **Chartered** 1978.

Chartered to support Naval Party 1007 at Aberdeen, *Clansman* is RFA-manned with specialist RN personnel aboard (hence her inclusion here). She is well equipped with the latest technology systems for diving (including a moonpool, stern ramp and decompression chamber), fire-fighting and anti-pollution work. She is owned by Seaforth Maritime and is of a design used for the support of North and Norwegian Sea offshore platforms.

Seaforth Clansman *underway* (RN/FPU).

TRAINING CRAFT
'Tracker' Class

Name *Attacker*; **Pennant number** P281; **Displacement** 34 tons; **Length** 19.5 m; **Beam** 5.2 m; **Draught** 1.5 m; **Propulsion** 2 × General Electric V12 diesels (1,300 shp), 2 × shafts; **Range** 650 nm at 12 kt; **Speed** 21 kt; **Complement** 2 officers and 9 ratings; **Sensors** 1 × Racal commercial; **Armament** 1 × 20 mm Oerlikon GP (not fitted); **Builders** Fairey Marine; **Commissioned** 11 March 1983; Attached to Strathclyde University (Clyde RNR).

Name *Chaser*; **Pennant number** P282; **Commissioned** 11 March 1983; Attached to Aberdeen University (Tay RNR).

Name *Fencer*; **Pennant number** P283; **Commissioned** 21 March 1983; Attached to Southampton University (Solent RNR).

Bottom *First of a new class of fast training craft for the Royal Naval Reserve and University Training units is* Attacker *(Mike Lennon).*

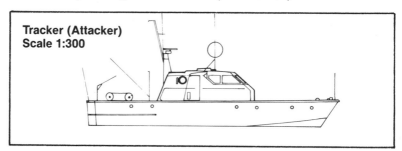

Tracker (Attacker)
Scale 1:300

Pictured in April 1986, Loyal Explorer *wears the blue ensign of the Royal Naval Auxiliary Service (RNXS) when entering Portsmouth* (Mike Lennon).

Name *Hunter*; **Pennant number** P284; **Commissioned** 21 March 1983; Attached London RNR.

Name *Striker*; **Pennant number** P285; **Commissioned** 21 March 1983; Attached to Liverpool University (Mersey RNR).

The 'Tracker' class of coastal training craft was introduced to take over the navigation and seamanship training roles of several types of small vessel used by British universities and the Royal Naval Reserve, and are based on a commercial design built at Cowes (*Attacker*) and Southampton. Armament is only fitted in wartime.

'Watercraft' P2000 Class

Name *Archer*; **Pennant number** P264; **Displacement** 43 tons; **Length (overall)** 20.8 m; **Beam** 5.8 m; **Draught** 1.5 m; **Propulsion** 2 × Rolls-Royce/ Perkins 12V MBT diesels (1,380 bhp); **Range** 500 nm at 15 kt; **Speed** 20 kt; **Complement** 14; **Sensors** Racal commercial; **Armament** 1 × 20 mm Oerlikon GAM-B01 (when fitted); **Builders** Watercraft (Shoreham); **Commissioned** 9 August 1985.

Others *Biter* (P270); *Smiter* (P272); *Purser* (P273); *Blazer* (P279); *Dasher* (P280); *Puncher* (P291); *Charger* (P292); *Ranger* (P293) and *Trumpeter* (P294). For RNXS service: *Loyal Example* (P153); *Loyal Explorer* (P154); *Loyal Express* (P163) and *Loyal Exploit* (P167).

On delivery to the Royal Navy is the Watercraft P2000 training craft, Archer (Watercraft Ltd).

A class of 14 patrol/training craft ordered from a successful British yard for the Royal Naval Reserve and the Royal Naval Auxiliary Service (RNXS). The craft were delivered monthly from August 1985.

'Bird' Class

Name *Peterel*; **Pennant number** P262; **Displacement** 190 tons; **Length (overall)** 36.6 m; **Beam** 7 m; **Draught** 2 m; **Propulsion** 2 × Paxman diesels (4,200 bhp), 2 × shafts; **Range** 2,000 nm at 14 kt; **Speed** 21 kt; **Complement** 4 officers and 19 ratings or cadets; **Armament** 1 × 40 mm Bofors GP Mk 9, 2 × 7.62 mm GPMG; **Sensors** 1 × 1006; **Builders** Richard Dunston; **Laid down** 1976; **Launched** 14 May 1976; **Completed** 1977; **Commissioned** 7 February 1977.

Name *Sandpiper*; **Pennant number** P263; **Laid down** 1976; **Launched** 20 January 1977; **Completed** 1977; **Commissioned** 16 September 1977.

Designed for Inshore Patrol work with the Fisheries Protection Squadron, the 'Bird' Class has been split into two groups, two craft being used for Northern Island blockade patrol and two as tenders to the Britannia Royal Naval College, Dartmouth for cadet and Midshipman seamanship and navigation training tasks. Both have an enclosed upper bridge.

Sandpiper *is a tender for BRNC Dartmouth* (HMS *Osprey*).

NAVAL SENSORS AND SONARS

In the preceeding pages various naval radars and other sensors have been mentioned in data panels, and are identified here in terms of their specific purposes. Details of missiles can be found in the companion volume in this series, *British Military Missiles*, by Paul Beaver and Terry Gander.

Sensors

Type	Purposes	Status
278	Height finding	Obsolescent
901	Fire control (Seaslug)	Obsolescent
903/904	Fire control (Seacat/114 mm)	In service
909	Fire control (Sea Dart)	In service
910	Fire control (Sea Wolf)	In service
911	Fire control (Sea Wolf)	Entering service
912	Fire control (Seacat/114 mm)	In service
965	Air search	Obsolescent
967/968	Surveillance	In service
975	Navigation	Obsolescent
978	Navigation	Obsolescent
992	Surveillance	In service
993/994	Air/surface search	In service
996	Long-range search	Entering service
1003	Navigation	In service
1006	Navigation	In service
1007	Navigation	Entering service
1022	Air/surface search	In service

Sonars

162	Classification	Obsolescent
170	Hull-mounted	Obsolescent
177	Medium range	Obsolescent
183	Submarine	In service
184	Medium range	Obsolescent
193/193M	Minehunting	In service
197	Submarine	In service
199	Variable depth	In service
2001	Submarine	In service
2007	Submarine	In service
2008	Hull-mounted	Entering service
2016	Medium range	In service

Type	Purposes	Status
2020	Submarine	In service
2024	Submarine TA	In service
2031	Escort TA	In service
2040	Submarine	Entering service
2050	Medium range	Entering service
2051	Submarine	Entering service
2093	Minehunting	Entering service

ROYAL NAVAL AIRCRAFT
British Aerospace Sea Harrier FRS 1

Purpose Shipborne STOVL strike fighter; **Crew** 1 pilot; **Squadrons** 800, 801, 899; **Range** 1,400 km; **Endurance** 2.4 hours; **Max speed** 625 kt (1,158 km/h); **Cruising speed** 485 kt (898 km/h); **Service ceiling** 35,000 ft (10,668 m); **Length (overall)** 14.5 m; **Length (folded)** 12.9 m; **Height** 3.7 m; **Span** 7.7 m; **Sensors** Ferranti Blue Fox, digital nav-attack, TACAN, RWR; **Weapons** 2 × 30 mm Aden cannon, 4 × AIM-9L Sidewinder air-to-air missiles, flares, chaff, Cluster bombs, 4 × 1,000 lb (454 kg), 2 × Sea Eagle anti-ship missile, nuclear weapons; **Engine** 1 ×Rolls-Royce Pegasus 104; **All-up weight** 10,433 kg.

Bottom *One of the most important roles for the embarked Sea Harrier FRS 1 fighters in the 'Invincible' Class CVSs is to intercept and identify shadowing aircraft like this Soviet Bear-E, intercepted by Lieutenant Alistair McLaren, RN, of 800 Squadron* (RN/800 Squadron).

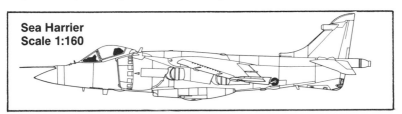

Sea Harrier
Scale 1:160

Westland Lynx HAS 2/3

Purpose Shipborne ASW/ASVW helicopter; **Crew** 1 pilot, 1 observer, up to 10 passengers; **Squadrons** 702, 815; **Range** 320 nm (593 km); **Endurance** 2.8 hours; **Max speed** 135 kt (250 km/h); **Cruising speed** 125 kt (232 km/h); **Single engine speed** 122 kt (226 km/h); **Service ceiling** 9,580 ft (2,920 m); **Length (fuselage)** 11.92 m; **Length (rotors turning)** 15.16 m; **Height** 3.58 m; **Width (fuselage)** 2.95 m; **Rotor diameter** 12.8 m; **Sensors** Ferranti Sea Spray Mk1/Mk3, Racal MIR-2, GEC Avionics PIDS (to be fitted); **Weapons** 2 × Mk 44, 2 × Mk 46 or 2 × Stingray torpedoes; 4 × Sea Skua anti-ship missiles; 2 × nuclear depth bombs; 2 × Mk 11 depth charges; 1 × 7.62 mm GPMG; **Engines** 2 × Rolls-Royce Gem; **All-up weight** 4,309 kg.

Bottom *Lynx HAS 2 from Liverpool Flight carrying four BAe Sea Skua missiles for anti-shipping tasks* (British Aerospace).

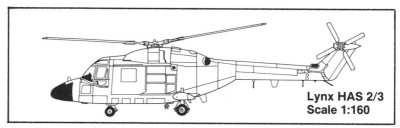

Lynx HAS 2/3
Scale 1:160

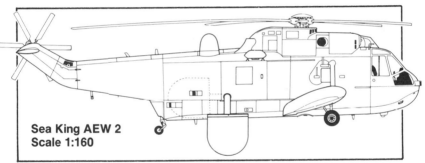

Sea King AEW 2
Scale 1:160

Top *A Sea King AEW 2 of 849A Flight, flown by Lieutenant Mark Watson, RN, seen over* Illustrious (RN/HMS *Illustrious*).

Westland Sea King AEW 2

Purpose Shipborne airborne early warning platform; **Crew** 1 pilot, 2 observers; **Squadrons** 849 (two flights); **Range** 420 nm (778 km); **Endurance** 4.25 hours; **Max speed** 110 kt (204 km/h); **Cruising speed** 90 kt (167 km/h); **Service ceiling** 10,000 ft (3,048 m); **Length (fuselage)** 14.4 m; **Length (rotors turning)** 22.15 m; **Height** 5.13 m; **Width (fuselage)** 5 m; **Rotor diameter** 18.9 m; **Sensors** Thorn-EMI Searchwater, Racal MIR-2, Cossor Jubilee Guardsman; **Engines** 2 × Rolls-Royce Gnome; **All-up weight** 9,707 kg.

Westland Sea King HAS 5

Purpose Shipborne medium ASW helicopter; **Crew** 2 pilots, 1 observer, 1 sonar operator; **Squadrons** 706, 810, 814, 819, 820, 824, 826; **Range** 664 nm (1,230 km); **Endurance** 5 hours; **Max speed** 112 kt (207 km/h); **Cruising speed** 100 kt (185 km/h); **Service ceiling** 10,600 ft (3,200 m); **Length (fuselage)** 17.01 m; **Length (rotors turning)** 22.15 m; **Height** 5.13 m; **Width (fuselage)** 5 m; **Rotor diameter** 18.9 m; **Sensors** MEL Sea/Super Searcher, Racal MIR-2; **Armament** 4 × Mk 44, 4 × Mk 46, or 4 × Stingray torpedoes; 4 × Mk 11 depth charges or nuclear depth bombs; 1 × 7.62 mm GPMG; **Engines** 2 × Rolls-Royce Gnome; **All-up weight** 9,526 kg.

Bottom *The Sea King HAS 5 is currently the most effective medium ASW helicopter in the world; this helicopter is carrying four Mk46 torpedoes and MAD (RN).*

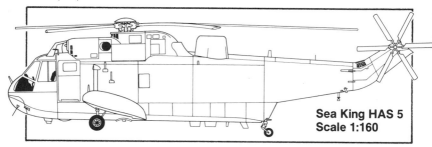

Sea King HAS 5
Scale 1:160

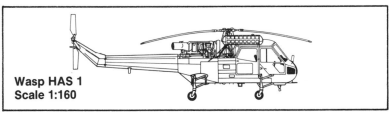

Wasp HAS 1
Scale 1:160

Top *Wasp HAS 1 — the helicopter will be phased out by 1988* (RN).

Westland Wasp HAS 1

Purpose Shipborne ASW/ASVW helicopter; **Crew** 1 pilot, 1 aircrewman; **Squadrons** 829 (disbanding late 1986); **Range** 415 nm (770 km); **Endurance** 2.4 hours; **Max speed** 120 kt (222 km/h); **Cruising speed** 100 kt (185 km/h); **Service ceiling** 12,600 ft (3,810 m); **Length (fuselage)** 7.85 m; **Length (rotors turning)** 12.29 m; **Height** 3.61 m; **Width (fuselage)** 2.64 m; **Rotor diameter** 9.83 m; **Sensor** Direct View SFIM sight; **Weapons** 2 x Mk 44 or Mk 46; 4 × Nord AS 12 anti-ship missiles, 2 × Mk 11 depth bombs or nuclear charges; 1 × 7.62 mm GPMG, flares, chaff; **Engine** 1 × Rolls-Royce Nimbus; **All-up weight** 2,457 kg.

Westland Wessex HU 5

Purpose General utility helicopter; **Crew** 1/2 pilots, 1 aircrewman, up to 16 passengers; **Squadrons** 771, 772, 845 (converting to Sea King HC 4 in 1986/87); **Range** 270 nm (500 km); **Endurance** 2.25 hours; **Max speed** 132 kt (245 km/h); **Cruising speed** 100 kt (185 km/h); **Service ceiling** 5,500 ft (1,676 m); **Length (fuselage)** 14.7 m; **Length (rotors turning)** 20.04 m; **Height** 4.93 m; **Width (fuselage)** 3.7 m; **Rotor diameter** 17.07 m; **Weapons** 1 × 7.62 mm GPMG, 2 × 68 mm rocket launcher pods, flares, chaff; **Engines** 2 × Rolls-Royce Gnome; **All-up weight** 6,120 kg.

Future aircraft for the Fleet Air Arm include the British Aerospace Sea Harrier FRS 2 (1989), the E.H. Industries EH 101 (from 1991) and the Westland Lynx HAS 8 (from 1988); full details of these types are still awaited.

The Westland Wasp HAS 1 and the Westland Wessex HU 5 will have been phased out of front line service by 1988.

Bottom *Royal Navy ground personnel prepare a Wessex 5 helicopter for operations in northern Norway* (MoD).

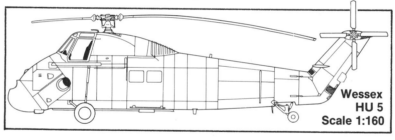

Wessex HU 5
Scale 1:160

INDEX OF VESSELS

Page numbers in **bold** represent photographs.

Abdiel, **96**
Achilles, *60*
Active, *64,* **66,** *67*
Ajax, *55*
Alacrity, *64,* **67**
Alderney, **104,** *105*
Amazon, *63,* **65**
Ambuscade, *64,* **66**
Andromeda, *61*
Anglesey, *105*
Antelope, *64, 67*
Apollo, *60*
Arethusa, *54*
Archer, *123,* **124/5**
Ardent, *64, 67*
Argonaut, **58**
Ariadne, *60*
Ark Royal, 8, **12,** *33*
Arrow, *64,* **70**
Arun, *94*
Athestone, *82*
Attacker, **122,** *123*
Aurora, *52,* **54**
Avenger, *64*

Bacchante, *60*
Battleaxe, *68*
Beagle, *114*
Beaver, **71,** *74,* **77**
Berkeley, *83*
Berwick, *52*
Bicester, *82*
Birmingham, *41,* **42/3**
Biter, *123*
Blackwater, *94*
Blazer, *123*
Bloodhound, *see* London
Bossington, *87*
Boxer, *74,* **76,** *77*
Brave, *74, 76, 77*
Brazen, *73,* **74**
Brecon, *82,* **83,** *84*
Brereton, *87*
Brighton, *52*
Brilliant, **68,** *73*
Brinton, *87*
Bristol, **37,** *38*
Broadsword, **68**
Brocklesby, *82*
Bronington, **72,** *87*

Bulldog, *114*

Campletown, *78*
Cardiff, *44*
Carron, *92,* **93**
Cattistock, *82*
Challenger, **118,** *119*
Charger, *123*
Charybdis, **FC,** **61,** *62*
Chaser, *123*
Chatham, *78*
Chiddingfold, *82,* **86**
Churchill, *23,* **24,** *25*
Cleopatra, *58*
Conqueror, *23,* **24,** *35*
Cornwall, *78*
Cottesmore, *83*
Courageous, *23*
Coventry, *47,* **76**
Crichton, *90*
Cumberland, *78*
Cumbria, *see* Cumberland
Cuxton, *89*
Cygnet, **109,** *110*

Danae, **56,** **69**
Dasher, *123*
Devonshire, *80*
Dido, *55*
Diomede, *60*
Dovey, *92*
Dulverton, *82*
Dumbarton Castle, *98*

Edinburgh, *50*
Endurance, *98,* **99**
Euryalus, *53,* **55**
Exeter, *44,* **45**

Falmouth, *52*
Fawn, *114,* **115**
Fearless, **13,** *34*
Fencer, *123*
Fife, **38,** *40*
Fox, *114*

Galatea, *55*
Gavinton, *88*
Glamorgan, **39,** *40*
Glasgow, *44*
Glasserton, *90*
Gleaner, *116,* **117**
Gloucester, **36,** *70*
Guardian, *106,* **107,** *110*

Guernsey, *105*

Hecate, *111*
Hecla, *111*
Helford, *92*
Helmsdale, *94*
Herald, *112,* **113**
Hermoine, *62, 63*
Hubberston, **87**
Humber, *92*
Hunter, *123*
Hurworth, *82*
Hydra, *111,* **112**

Illustrious, 8, **9,** *33*
Intrepid, *14,* **15**
Invincible, 8
Itchen, *94*
Iveston, *87*

Jersey, *104*
Juno, *56,* **57**
Jupiter, **62,** *70*

Kedleston, *88*
Kellington, *88*
Kingfisher, *110*
Kirliston, *89*

Leander, *55*
Ledbury, **71,** *82,* **84/5**
Leeds Castle, **72,** *98,* **100**
Lindisfarne, *105*
Liverpool, **46,** *47*
London, *76*
Londonderry, *52*
Lowestoft, *52*
Loyal Explorer, *123*
Loyal Exploit, *123*
Loyal Express, *123*

Manchester, **48/9,** *50*
Maxton, *89*
Middleton, *83*
Minerva, *55*

Naiad, *54,* **69**
Newcastle, **41,** *44*
Norfolk, *80*
Nottingham, *44,* **46**
Nurton, **88**

Oberon, *29,* **BC**
Ocelet, **29**
Odin, **27**

Olympus, *27*
Onslaught, *27*
Onyx, **28**, *29*
Opportune, *29*
Opossum, **30**, *31*
Oracle, *29*
Orkney, *104*
Orpheus, *29*
Orwell, *94*
Osiris, *27*
Otter, *29, 31*, **35**
Otus, **28**

Peacock, **101**
Penelope, *55, 56*
Peterel, *110, 126*
Phoebe, **45**, *57, 58*
Plover, *103*
Plymouth, *52*
Protector, **106**, *110*
Puncher, *123*

Ranger, *123*
Redpole, *110*
Renown, *16*, **17**
Repulse, *16*
Resolution, *16*, **18**
Revenge, *16*

Rhyl, *52*
Ribble, *94*
Roebuck, *114*
Rothesay, *51*

Sandown, *94*, **95**
Sandpiper, *110*, **126**
Sceptre, *21*
Scylla, *62, 63*
Seaforth Clansman, *119*, **120/1**
Sentinel, *107*, **108**, *110*
Sheffield, *47, 76*
Sheraton, *89*
Shetland, *105*
Sirius, *58*
Smiter, *123*
Southampton, *44*, **45**
Sovereign, *21*
Spartan, *21*
Spey, *94*
Splendid, *21*, **22**
Starling, *103*
Striker, *123*
Superb, *21*, **23**
Swallow, *103*
Swift, *103*
Swiftsure, *21*, **22, 34**

Talent, *19*
Tireless, *19*
Torbay, *19*
Torquay, *57*
Trafalgar, **19**, *20*
Trenchant, *19*
Triumph, *19*
Trumpeter, *123*
Turbulent, *19*, **20**

Unicorn, *32*
Unseen, *32*
Upholder, *31*, **32**
Upton, **89**
Ursula, *32*

Valiant, *25, 26*
Vanguard, *18*

Warspite, *25*, **26**
Waveney, *92*, **93**
Wilton, *83, 90*, **91**, *92*
Wooton, **90**

Yarmouth, *52*
York, **36**, *50*